ADVERTISING

ITS PLACE IN POLITICAL AND MANAGERIAL ECONOMICS

ADVERTISING

ITS PLACE IN POLITICAL AND
MANAGERIAL ECONOMICS

W. Duncan Reekie

Lecturer, Department of Business Studies,
University of Edinburgh

Macmillan

First published 1974 by
THE MACMILLAN PRESS LTD
London and Basingstoke
Associated companies in New York
Dublin Melbourne Johannesburg and Madras

SBN 333 15458 4

Typeset in Great Britain by
PREFACE LIMITED
Salisbury, Wilts
and printed by
LEWIS REPRINTS LTD
Member of Brown Knight and Truscott Ltd
London and Tonbridge

To Jenny and Ruth

Hullabaloo, a means of swindling the people and foisting upon them goods frequently useless or of dubious value.

The Russian Encyclopaedia, 1941

The popularisation of goods with the aim of selling them, the creation of demand for these goods, the acquaintance of consumers with their quality, particular features and the location of their sales, and explanation of the methods of their use.

The Great Soviet Encyclopaedia, 1972

Contents

Preface and Acknowledgements

Advertising is an important and controversial subject. It is of interest to economists, politicians, businessmen and sociologists. This book is aimed at meeting the needs of the first three of these groupings. Academically the level of the book is that of the second or third year in an undergraduate economics or business studies course. But it should also be of value to postgraduate business school students, and, of course, to advertisers themselves, and to politicians with a particular interest in the subject.

Early drafts of this book were read and commented on by various people. In particular, helpful advice was obtained from Professor Harry Townsend and Mr George Polanyi. To both these scholars I owe a debt of gratitude. Any errors which remain in this text are, of course, my own responsibility.

Finally, my thanks are due to my wife Ruth, who encouraged me in my task over many nights and weekends, while simultaneously performing the nearly impossible job of transcribing my handwriting into type. During this time she also carried on her normal work as a general practitioner, and only when the task was completed did she give up typing and medicine to produce, with perfect synchronisation, the first member of our family.

W.D.R.

1 Introduction

Advertising has long been a fascinating socio-political topic. In the United States the Federal Trade Commission has devoted considerable effort to learn more about the subject by holding (in 1971) extensive 'Hearings on Modern Advertising Practices'. In Britain the Labour Party has recently produced a Green Paper (1) devoted solely to the impact of advertising on the economy and on society. After the Monopolies Commission report on detergent advertising in 1966 (2) the then Board of Trade launched a wider investigation into the effects of advertising throughout the economy and across industry boundaries.

Certainly advertising both poses problems and evokes controversy. This book examines some of the more important of these problems and controversies. In parts an attempt is merely made to put the issues in perspective. In the bulk of the book, however, use is made of the principles of microeconomic theory to arrive at normative conclusions.

Plan and Purpose of the Book

The book falls into three distinct, but associated areas: first (chapters 2 and 3), historical and social; second (chapters 4

and 5), economic and commercial at the level of the firm;
third (chapters 6, 7 and 8), economic and political at the
level of the national economy.

Chapter 2 provides a brief account of, and a rationale for,
the history of advertising and its current conspicuous
position in modern society. The arguments which this
obtrusiveness has aroused are detailed. Chapter 3 provides an
examination of the social and ethical views which have gone
to make up these arguments. Charges that advertising is
untruthful and in bad taste are examined and the frequently
made claim that it makes people want what they do not
really need is discussed.

One of the major economic criticisms of advertising is that
it is excessive. The group of people with one of the strongest
motivations to prevent advertising rising beyond a worthwhile level is the business community itself. Profit-maximising self-interest on the part of businessmen will tend to
ensure that advertising is not carried beyond that point where
the last pound spent on advertising brings in less than one
pound of extra revenue. This may explain why relative
advertising expenditure has 'peaked off' in the last decade.
Businessmen may be realising that advertising has reached a
point of diminishing marginal net revenues. The discussion in
Chapter 4 does not refute this possibility, but views it with
pessimism since management techniques are still largely rule
of thumb in nature. However, Chapter 5 suggests that the
optimising thinking which lies behind economic analysis can
increasingly be used in management decision taking. The
conceptual tools of marginal analysis are described in
Chapters 4 and 5, and in the latter chapter, a means of
applying the principles of marginal equivalency to advertising
decisions is put forward.

Chapters 5 and 7 describe the market for advertising.
Conceptually advertisers can be seen as *suppliers* of information, and the public as *demanders* for information about the
goods they intend to consume. The demand conditions and
supply conditions which exist in this market are enumerated
and evaluated. While this helps to clarify thought as to where
the equilibrium position of supply and demand should lie, it
must be conceded that the suspicion that advertising is 'too

high' cannot be wholly refuted. If so, this can result in, *inter alia*, barriers to entry, and thus high prices, waste of resources, ill-founded claims and so on.

Chapter 8 examines a number of policy alternatives which might improve the operation of the market in advertising and so curb any excess or waste which exists. The role of the Monopolies Commission is assessed; the possible impact of levying a tax on advertising is examined; possible self-policing by the industry is discussed; and finally, an evaluation is made of the worth of increasing the flow of information to consumers to encourage greater discernment in both the purchasing of products and the 'consumption' of advertisements.

Chapter 9 is principally concerned with summarising the main thesis of the preceding chapters. Attention is also drawn, in this final chapter, to the views of those who, like Toynbee and Galbraith, abhor many of the aspects of life in modern developed economies and who suspect that advertising is a major contributor to the form of society they dislike. Lastly, the chapter puts forward suggested lines for further discussion in a debate which is far from ended.

2 From Conception to Maturity

Since Eve first displayed her charms to Adam, advertising has been with us. The streets of ancient Rome were filled with barkers. Restoration London saw criers call out the merits of their wares, though few could have had the appeal and impact of the orange seller, Nell Gwynn. The apocryphal Molly Malone strode through Dublin with 'cockles and mussells, alive, alive-o'.

The printed word joined the spoken in advertising at least as early as the eighteenth century. The *Spectator* newspaper was used as a medium in 1710. An issue in that year advertised:

An Incomparable Powder for cleaning Teeth,
which has given great satisfaction to most
of the Nobility and Gentry in England.

Later that same century, Dr Samuel Johnson remarked that 'the trade of advertising is now so near perfection that it is not easy to propose any improvement'. Whatever the accuracy of this statement, Johnson could not have been expected to foresee the tremendous impact which the

Industrial Revolution would have on society and, in turn, on the nature, if not the 'perfection' of advertising.

1. The Development of the Mass Market

The Industrial Revolution and the techniques of mass production which developed from it reached full flower in the manufacture of Henry Ford's Model T. The Model T was the epitome of the success of the Industrial Revolution. Ford's achievement was due to one main selling point, lowness of price, coupled with a lack of similar, inexpensive products in the past. Prior to the Model T, the individual seeking a cheap, personal transportation system had to invest in a horse and buggy, a product which could hardly be called the most satisfactory of substitutes, and one which, in any event, would be manufactured on a custom-built, one-off, high-cost basis at the local coachbuilders. The poor were thus precluded from owning their own personal transport, and only the very rich could contract out of the disadvantages associated with horse-drawn vehicles, by buying the very costly products of Benz and Royce.

Ford's low price depended on standardisation of product, and uniformity of assembly technique. These are the basic components of mass production technology. Mass production depends in turn on a mass market to absorb the output. In Ford's case the mass market was made possible by mass communication about the product and by its attractively low price. So the circle was completed and advertising's place in it seemingly defined.

2. The Development of the Marketing Concept

Scope for further change in the nature and extent of advertising had to wait until later in the twentieth century. In the U.S.A. the change can possibly be dated to the early twenties. The days when lowness of price and uniformity of product were sufficient to sell a product were ending. ('You can have any colour you want, so long as it's black,' growled Old Henry.) Incomes were rising, people no longer had to buy the cheapest, black car as a form of transport. They could afford to exercise their preferences for something different, or defer purchase till a satisfactory product became

available. In the automobile trade, General Motors willingly
obliged by producing coloured Chevrolets. The disastrous
results for Ford, of failing to comply with the market's needs,
are too well known to require detailed recounting here.
Suffice to say that, by 1946, Ford was turning in losses of
$10 million each month.

So the marketing concept was born. Firms became aware
that to stay in business it was not sufficient to produce a
well-engineered product, then try to sell it. The market had
to be studied, its varying wants assessed, and then a product,
or products, tailored to meet them. Figure 2.1 conceptualises
this change from product orientation to market orientation:
The firm's entire way of thinking is reversed.

Fig. 2.1

In the United Kingdom this change in approach to
marketing possibly occurred rather later than in the U.S.A.
The apparently high standards of living in the U.S.A. in the
twenties did not exist at the mass level in Britain in those
years. Personal incomes, on which the ability to exercise
individual preferences in the market-place depends, did not
stand much above an austerity level until the impact of World
War II was left behind. From around 1950, however, British
standards of living also began to rise beyond the level where
price and utility were the main criteria for purchase.

Mass production required mass communication through
the mass media to obtain the turnover required for low-cost
production. Yet, according to the marketing concept, this
alone is an insufficient prescription for success. The mass
communication must relate to a product which the market
has an overt or latent need for, and be carried out in a style
which attracts, rather than offends, the people at which it is
aimed. In so far as the marketing concept has been adopted,

and in so far as customer orientation and appeal are the aim, the question is begged as to why advertising should have attracted the exceptional odium it did in the fifties and sixties.

The critical writings of Packard (1) and Galbraith (2, 3) for example, are too well known to require additional publicity here. Why did their books receive massive public acclaim? It was not because of the advent of advertising for the first time; not because mass communication was being used for the first time; not because modern advertising's many faults (which were being attacked long before Packard and Galbraith did so) were appearing for the first time. Probably there are many reasons, of which the following three causes are among the most important:

(a) The rate of growth of advertising expenditure.
(b) The advent of TV.
(c) The growth of self-service retailing.

3. The Increasing Depersonalisation of Selling

These three points will now be examined at greater length. Table 2.1 shows how advertising expenditure in the U.K. has more than quadrupled between 1952 and 1971. A comparison less distorted by inflation is advertising's share of gross national product (GNP). This increased by half, rising from 0.9 per cent in 1952 to 1.4 per cent in 1960. Throughout the sixties, however, advertising's share of GNP remained fairly constant, falling slightly, to 1.2% by 1971. Comparative data for the U.S.A. show advertising's share of GNP rising from 1.6 per cent in 1946 to 2.4 per cent in 1956. As in the United Kingdom, this rise was followed by a levelling off and slight fall to 2.2 per cent in 1966. (4)

So, in real terms, advertising became more obtrusive in the fifties then it had ever been before. This increased obtrusiveness can certainly be argued to have been one of the factors encouraging increased discussion and heightened disapproval of the activity. Simultaneously, however, a new advertising medium appeared — the television set. Magazine advertisements can be ignored by turning a page, TV advertisements have a certain hypnotic compulsiveness. The control knobs of

Table 2.1. *Total advertising expen-*
diture and its relation to con-
sumers' expenditure and GNP.

Year	Total expenditure £ m	Total expenditure as a percentage of	
		Consumers' expenditure	GNP
1952	123	1.2	0.9
1956	197	1.4	1.1
1960	323	1.9	1.4
1961	338	1.9	1.4
1962	348	1.8	1.4
1963	371	1.8	1.4
1964	416	1.9	1.4
1965	435	1.9	1.4
1966	447	1.8	1.4
1967	458	1.8	1.3
1968	503	1.8	1.4
1969	544	1.9	1.4
1970	554	1.8	1.3
1971	591	1.7	1.2

Source: Advertising Quarterly, 32 (1972).

the set are several feet away from the viewer, who, in any
event, is awaiting the main programme. 'What might be
acceptable and even entertaining in a newspaper advertisement . . . might seem intrusive and undesirable when inserted
into entertainment programmes in the home.' (5) The notion
of an electronic goggle-box advising people what to purchase
as they sat in their own living-rooms proved too much for
some writers, and the criticism increased.

This decreasing humanisation of the marketing process was
accompanied by the rapid demise in the fifties and sixties
(earlier in the U.S.A.), of the traditional retailer. Face-to-face
conversations with one's neighbourhood grocer became the
exception rather than the rule, and self-service shopping
became the vogue. In 1947 only ten grocery shops were
self-service. According to the *Nielsen Researcher* this figure
had risen to 28,062 by 1969. As late as 1965, 55 per cent of
grocery sales still went through counter service shops. By
1969, the figure had slumped to 36 per cent.

Manufacturer ⇄ Wholesaler ⇄ Retailer ⇄ Consumer

Fig. 2.2a. *The traditional distribution channel*

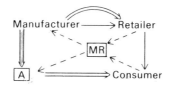

Manufacturer ——→ Retailer

MR

A ⇐⇐⇐⇐⇒ Consumer

———→ Flow of goods
═══⇒ Flow of advertising messages
← – – – Feedback of market and consumer information
A   Advertising specialists
MR   Market research specialists

Fig. 2.2b. *The distribution channel as it is tending to become*

The effect which this had on marketing methods and on the shopper is conceptualised in Figs. 2.2a and 2.2b. The era of salesmanship and face-to-face selling is disappearing from all stages of the distribution channel. In the past, products were 'pushed' through the channel by the manufacturer's salesmen approaching a wholesaler, whose sales force in turn sold to retailers, who, in their turn, recommended purchase to (often personally known) individual customers (Fig. 2.2a). Now, the selling effort is primarily directed at the final consumer (Fig. 2.2b). The various mass media are often used for this purpose, face-to-face recommendation has no place in the self-service situation, and the goods are 'pulled' by consumers through the channel. The alert retailer must stock the items which consumers have chosen from those listed in the adverts they have seen.

Rising advertising outlays *per se*, however, are not enough on which to build a case against the activity. To do so on that basis alone is as logical as condemning or condoning a rise in expenditure on annual holidays or a rise in the crime rate. The rise may or may not be socially and economically justifiable. Further and deeper investigation is required before a stance can be adopted as to what is the 'correct' level of advertising.

To condemn the activity because TV is now used as a medium is as illogical as confusing the respective merits of the singer and the song. TV is a method of communication, advertising is one facet of the activity of communicating. The question is not whether society can cope with advertising but whether it can cope with the problems posed, and the advantages brought, by television.

In like manner, advertising should not be condemned because of the advent of mass distribution. Mass distribution may or may not be a good thing, but advertising is a neutral agent which could just as readily be used to hinder its spread as it is to encourage it. Advertising deserves to be examined in a wider context than merely that of the last twenty years, and it deserves to be judged on its merits, not on the attractiveness or repulsiveness of associated phenomena. What then is the field of battle which should be chosen for this wider debate?

4. The Great Debate

Advertising frequently generates controversy. No one is unaware of the activity. Most people hold opinions on the subject. Some praise, some condemn, still others use it as a basis for humour, cynical or good natured. But most would agree, that for better or for worse, advertising is a vigorous and ubiquitous means of communication.

We have seen, that like the poor, advertising has always been with us. It is not a new phenomenon. Yet the extent of its usage, its sheer social obtrusiveness, seems — certainly at a casual glance — to be inversely related to poverty. Modern economic growth, as understood in capitalist countries using mass production technology, has a strong relationship with a high level of advertising.

This relationship prompted Sir Winston Churchill to write that 'advertising nourishes the consuming power of men. It creates wants for a better standard of living . . . It spurs individual exertion and greater production.' (6) The opposite view was taken by the historian Arnold Toynbee. He wrote, 'If this [relationship] were demonstrated to be true, it would also demonstrate, to my mind, that an economy of abundance is a spiritually unhealthy way of life.' (7)

Most supporters of advertising adopt some variant of the Churchillian argument. The assumption is made that there is some sort of causal association between advertising and material welfare. Few critics of advertising, however, are as outspoken as Toynbee. Few are as willing to advocate, as he goes on to do, that the material standards of living of an American monk or nun would be preferable, without advertising, to existing living standards with advertising.

Toynbee may be right, and there may be great spiritual and moral benefits which the human race has forfeited by scorning the lack of material goals of a St Francis of Assisi. The remainder of this discussion, however, will be conducted on the assumption that mankind does want to better his material lot subject to the generally accepted moral and legal rules of the society of the day.

In this context the following charges are frequently made against the activity of advertising: (8)

(a) It leads to monopolistic situations and reduces price competition.
(b) It is higher than is necessary to communicate its message to its audience. As a result, costs — and also prices — are higher than they need be.
(c) It encourages firms to seek out unnecessary opportunities for product differentiation in order to provide tangible and obvious promotable points.
(d) It distorts consumer preferences, and results in faulty product evaluations.
(e) This results in a departure from the optimal resource allocation which can be argued to exist in a perfectly competitive situation with perfect information.
(f) It increases the amplitude of the business cycle.
(g) By its subsidisation of the media, it inhibits the freedom of the press and television.

On the other hand, it is often claimed that advertising can achieve the following benefits for society: (9)

(a) It facilitates the attainment of scale economies in production.

(b) It can reduce fluctuations in demand, so mopping up idle capacity.
(c) It can concentrate demand on fewer varieties thus reducing costs of excessive proliferation.
(d) Marketing costs are lower than, say, with salesmen.
(e) It can increase the flow of market information about entrant or existing firms, so making competition by price or product more effective.
(f) It provides through branding, an implicit quality guarantee, and so also stimulates improvement.
(g) It stimulates innovation.
(h) It facilitates diffusion of innovation.
(i) It widens consumer choice by making the range of options more widely known. It thus also raises the incentive to strive for a higher standard of living.
(j) By subsidising the mass media, it enables the general public to learn more about the world around them than otherwise they would if they had to purchase such information at a cost-related price.

Several of these alleged advantages are, of course, merely the obverse of the corresponding claimed disadvantages. For example, by subsidising the media, advertising provides the public with inexpensive access to valuable information. But, simultaneously, it removes the media's financial independence and so reduces the probability of the media being wholly unfettered in the opinions they hold. Similarly the claim that advertising can concentrate demand on fewer varieties is attractive so long as it results in cost reduction, but ceases to be so if it leads to reduced competition and monopoly pricing.

Thus the claims and counterclaims made for and against advertising are not mutually exclusive. Neither are they, if taken as a group, always internally consistent. It is not immediately apparent, for example, that its claimed ability to raise consumer choice by, among other things, increasing the rate of innovation is wholly reconcilable with its ability to concentrate demand on fewer varieties.

Nevertheless our task here is not to criticise these arguments as a group. Rather, it is to recognise that, over time, most of these viewpoints have been held by different people and that the debate which they engendered has yet to be settled. It is hoped that the next few chapters will make a positive contribution to that debate.

3 Social and Ethical Problems

Questioning the morality of advertising is not new. Many feel called to provide judgemental verdicts; few chose to give their opinions factual backing. Discussions on the subject tend to be long on persausive semantics but short on hard data. This is inevitable in any controversy over moral standards, which — by definition — are highly personal, highly subjective phenomena.

Five of the major controversies over advertising will be examined in this chapter. Is it in bad taste? It is excessive? Is it untruthful? Does it make people want what they do not really need? Does it hamper freedom of speech?

In a free society each individual is at liberty to hold whatever opinion on morality he pleases. The ensuing discussion attempts to present most of the varying and widely held opinions on advertising's moral role in society today.

1. Is Advertising in Bad Taste

This aspect of advertising can be subdivided into advertisement *content* and advertisement *location*.

Unscrupulous use of sex appeal in advertisements is one of

14

the most frequently cited examples of offensive advertising content. Clearly, for many products, the use of sex appeal is a highly relevant technique. It is easy to justify the relevance of a scantily clad, attractive girl in an advert for bikinis. It is less easy to do so if the same girl appears in an advert for cigars. Yet is lack of immediate relevance to the product advertised a suitable foundation on which to base a charge of offensiveness? Offensiveness means different things to different people. The National Viewers and Listeners Association so successfully sponsored by Mrs Mary Whitehouse has very strong views on the offensiveness of many TV programmes. These views are diametrically opposed to those of many TV producers and critics. The novel *Fanny Hill*, regarded by many as obscene, was 'enjoyed very much' by Marghanita Laski. What might be regarded as clever humour by a group of university students might be viewed as needlessly vulgar by an older age group.

A lack of consensus over 'bad taste' is endemic in society. It is not confined to the TV screen, or to the theatre, to literature, to art, or even to advertising. Rather, the lack of agreement is a function of our humanity. Given this, it is unreasonable to expect that advertisements will never contain material which somebody, somewhere, will judge to be in bad taste. Nevertheless it *is* reasonable for the public to expect the advertising industry to attempt to abide by generally accepted public standards of taste. This, in fact, the British Code of Advertising Practice* tries to ensure. For example, *inter alia*, it recommends that no advert should offend public decency, no advert should exploit the superstitious, and no advert should play on or appeal to fear as inducement to purchase the product advertised.

Advertisements are sometimes judged to be in bad taste, not because of their content, but because of their location. The dangers involved in pollution of the environment came to the forefront of public debate in the late sixties, and advertising has not escaped its share of the limelight. The atmosphere can be polluted by industrial fumes and by

*Discussed in more detail in Chapter 8.

motor-car exhausts. Rivers and lakes can, and have, been rendered undrinkable for humans and unfit for fish to live in due to sewage disposal and industrial waste discharge. The visual environment is despoiled by careless litter louts, by waste heaps of used cars *and* by advertisement hoardings. Again the problem is not one which is unique to advertising. The charge of bad taste which is levelled at large bill posters in countryside and town has its origins in opinions more broadly held throughout society than merely in any specific anti-advertising lobby. Two things are worth saying in this context. Firstly, the rise of the antipollution lobby, while possibly partly a reflection of increased environmental deterioration, is also a reflection of rising expectations on the part of the public. Rising living standards at the level of the consumption of private goods has led to expectations of a similar rise in the quality and quantity of public goods. For example, fish have been seen in the Thames under central London bridges in the last fifteen years, for the first time in over a century. The river is purer than it has been for a hundred years. (1)

Nonetheless public standards may have changed, and the Thames may still be regarded — in today's climate of opinion — as being unacceptably polluted. Similarly, bill hoardings which ten years ago received only, or possibly less then, the attention their sponsors desired, are today the object of criticism on the grounds of detracting from the natural beauties of the environment.

Secondly, given that advertising is not unique in being a target of the antipollution lobby, should the responsibility for any pollution it is alleged to cause be laid solely at the advertising industry's door? Should the motorist be held responsible for his exhaust fumes? Should the industrialist be held responsible for the waste he discharges into the river?

Clearly no industrialist will willingly assume the costs of preventing river pollution because this would make him less profitable than his rivals who did not adopt such measures. No motorist will go to the expense of rendering his car exhaust fumes pollution free, since environmental improvement will be miniscule if his fellow motorists do not follow suit. No advertiser will refrain from using bill hoardings, which, if rivals did not do likewise, would almost certainly result in lower sales.

The problem of visual offensiveness is merely a variant of the familiar problem of external costs. The full costs of motoring, river pollution, or hoarding advertisements are not borne by those who initiate or incur the actions. A substantial proportion of the costs 'spill over' and have to be absorbed by society at large. The only way to avoid this is by government action which can take the form of compelling people to bear the full costs of the activities they undertake; or by government subsidy to those members of the public who absorb the external costs; or, and possibly most practicably in the case of advertising, by prohibiting the activity which causes the offence.*

On the other hand, it could be argued that some bill hoardings serve a *positive* aesthetic function. Some are located to block or cover unattractive views, buildings, derelict sites or vacant shops. The Piccadilly Circus illuminated 'spectaculars' are a tourist attraction known the world over. Clearly no definitive answer can be given as to the bad taste or otherwise of a hoarding's location. The verdict must obviously depend on the merits of the individual case.

The location of adverts can also be condemned for being in poor taste when they interrupt the smooth flow of television viewing, magazine reading and so on. Some TV viewers, of course, would dispute this and claim that such breaks provide useful intervals during long programmes. Equally, many magazine readers undoubtedly gain considerable enjoyment from perusing advertisements, as well as from the feature articles themselves.

---

*It would be theoretically possible, for example, to recompense householders whose property loses value due to proximity to a bill hoarding. But there is large potential for disagreement on the level of subsidy, and anyway, other members of the community who are aesthetically offended but not directly economically damaged, cannot be recompensed in this way. The action taken could be either government subsidy or payment by the advertiser directly to the injured party. However, both approaches seem to suffer from potentially high administrative costs and overlarge scope for judgemental errors. Neither approach is particularly practicable.

18

Advertising

2. Is Advertising Excessive?

By its very nature, advertising is conspicuous. Few would deny that some is wasteful. As a result, one of the most pervasive of all causes of concern about advertising is its allegedly high absolute level. Many people think that overmuch time, money and resources are spent on it. This charge must be regarded seriously, and Chapters 6 and 7 are devoted to discussing those factors which can affect levels of advertising in the economy. These chapters show how difficult it is to establish what is meant by excess.

The task is made no easier by the fact that different industries can have widely differing advertising levels. On the face of it this might seem to indicate overexpenditure on advertising by some, and underexpenditure by others. But conditions of demand and supply can vary widely between industries, and even were they similar, advertising is only one of a range of substitutes which firms can choose to use to carry out the total task of marketing their commodities.

There is, for example, a high cross-elasticity of substitution between salesmen and advertising; between 'pushing' and 'pulling' goods through the distribution channel. Ice-cream is a product which tends to be pushed, detergents tend to be pulled, even where the manufacturer is the same firm. Table 3.1 shows the comparative total marketing costs of Unilever's detergent and ice-cream divisions. Relatively, detergent promotion is over two-and-a-half times as great as that of ice-cream. But the other marketing costs of ice-cream are nearly twice those of detergents.

Table 3.1. *Unilever's comparative marketing costs as a percentage of retail price*

	Detergents	Ice-cream
Advertising and other sales promotions	16	6
Other selling costs	8	20
Margin allowed to retailers	19	32
	43	58

Source: G. Polanyi, *Detergents: A Question of Monopoly*, IEA Research Monograph 24 (1970) 18.

3. Is Advertising Untruthful?

There is no doubt that untruthful advertisements have appeared in the press and on the TV screen. But so have untruthful statements been made by politicians, public figures, radio announcers, preachers, authors and private individuals. The responsibility for untruthfulness lies with the singer, not the song; with the advertis*er*, not with advertis*ing*.

Few would dispute that untruthful advertising should be prohibited in some way. One of the most effective deterrents to false or misleading claims is an educated or sceptical public. If an advert arouses a 'Who are you trying to kid?' response in its audience, it is unlikely that the advertiser will continue with a manifestly unsuccessful and untruthful campaign. Even if initial purchases are made, if a product does not measure up to the claims made for it, then no amount of advertising — however extravagant and untruthful — will persaude the aware consumer to make a repeat purchase of the unsatisfactory article.

Where consumers are less able to evaluate a product's properties against its claimed advantages, then a strong case for external control of advert content can be made. This explains the existence, for example, of the pharmaceutical industry's Code of Marketing Practice. Medicines are notoriously difficult to evaluate wholly objectively due to their so-called placebo effect. Medicines have been happy hunting-grounds for 'quack' doctors and for extravagant statements since earliest times. The therapeutic impact of even the most modern, scientifically tested drug may still owe something to the psychological implications of the placebo effect on the patient. As a result, medical advertising is open to abuse. This is why all the responsible pharmaceutical manufacturers have accepted the self-imposed restraint of the Code of Practice in order to reduce risks of such abuse and to deal with any lapses.

Is Persuasion Untruthful?

When people worry about the 'truthfulness' of advertising it is doubtful if it is blatant misrepresentation which is in the forefront of their minds. Rather, they are concerned with the degree to which advertising departs from the literal truth, the

degree to which the truth is 'stretched' and the degree to
which the advertiser employs what some might euphemistic-
ally call 'poetic licence'.

There is a widespread presumption that to use literal truth
in an advert is permissible but to move away from a position
of literal truth is, in some way, indictable. This was the
stance adopted by Professor Pigou when he distinguished
between 'informative' and 'competitive' advertising. (2) Competitive, or persausive advertising he saw as primarily designed to move demand from one firm to another. He
regarded persuasive advertising as wasteful, and thought that
the waste could be avoided by taxing or prohibition. (3)
Certainly, wildly extravagant claims have been made in
adverts. Few people would now defend the nineteenth-
century advert which showed the Pope on his throne in full
regalia, grasping a mug of Bovril, and headed, 'The two
infallible powers — the Pope and Bovril.' (4)

Even if one accepts that *persuasive* advertising is somehow
'bad' and *informative* advertising 'good', it is a false distinc-
tion. Isolating the one from the other is an impossible task.
The baldest statement of fact must still, in some way, be
persuasive. The persuasion may only take the form of a large
or striking use of typeface, but persuade it must, otherwise
the intended reader will not give up time from some other
action in order to absorb the message. A sign outside a
garage, which boldly informs passing motorists that it is the
'last filling station till Dartmoor', presents a very persuasive
case for purchasing petrol.

Advertising appeals to the emotions by using eloquent
phraseology, catchy music and attractive pictures or designs
to aid it in persuasion. It would be a foolish man who would
condemn eloquence, music and art as undesirable aspects of
society. That they have been used for undesirable ends is
undeniable. The question we need to ask ourselves is whether
the use of emotional appeals is or is not desirable when the
individual is in the purchase situation.

In so far as advertising is being judged in the purchase
situation alone* it should be judged on how it assists the

---

*It can also be judged on its ability to alter the production situation, as, for
example, when it leads to scale economies by expanding demand.

purchaser to decide between alternatives. Do adverts help the purchaser most when they are most informative and least persuasive or vice versa? An advert for a suit of clothes could tell a man that it is lightweight, hard wearing and composed of x per cent wool and y per cent synthetic fibres. An advert for perfume could tell a woman that the mixture has a volatility level of z per cent and that analysis would show a breakdown by chemical type of certain chlorates and carbons derived from specific botanic and animal matter.

Yet neither such listings of facts are wholly adequate in helping a man to choose a suit of clothes, or a woman a bottle of perfume. A man wants to look smart and stylish; a woman wants to feel attractive and glamorous. The ability of products to meet consumer needs for style and glamour cannot be conveyed through objective listings of facts; the advertiser must perforce resort to what Frank Knight once called 'industrial poetry'. (5)

When a man buys a suit he does not merely buy a piece of cloth tailored to cover his body. He buys a multiplicity of other satisfactions as well. He hopes to be smart and crisp looking in the presence of his friends, his colleagues at work and his family. If a man were merely *homus economicus* he would be content with the cheapest heat-conserving and wind- and water-repelling garment he could find. But man, as Veblen pointed out, is a social animal. (6) This may imply that he wants to identify with the culture or subculture of which he is a member, or alternatively, to identify with a reference group to which he aspires, but is not a member. In any event he will choose clothes at least partly to satisfy whatever particular social wants are most dominant in him as an individual. He will not be influenced by merely objective economic data. Thus the Burton 'Director' suit is not advertised solely for sale to company directors. The ethos of the adverts, however — the boardroom and chaffeur-driven car — vicariously link the wearer to the executive life. Conversely, Dunn and Co. advertise their menswear (1972) as having changeless, middle of the road, conservative, classic styling, the target market being the man who wants to look well groomed but not conspicuous.

When a woman buys a bottle of perfume she is not merely

buying a glass container full of a certain aromatic compound. She is purchasing a multiplicity of other satisfactions also. To quote a former president of Revlon Cosmetics: 'We sell hope.' A woman buying perfume is hoping to be attractive to men and noticeable to other women. If she were solely motivated by economic factors she would give up wearing cosmetics altogether. If she were solely motivated by social factors she would content herself with either the cheapest, most effective antiperspirant or deodorant, or possibly by just taking a hot bath. But women and men are motivated by factors other than economic, and other than the desire 'to belong', as suggested by Veblen. Men and women are motivated by *symbolic* as well as *economic–functional* product attributes. Kotler regards this as one of the major marketing implications of the development of the Freudian school of psychology. (7) At the very least, a bottle of perfume symbolises sexual attractiveness, as well as possessing qualities which can mitigate unpleasant body odours.

In a modern society few of our wants are related to the bare level of material subsistence. Most of our wants are, at the very least, coloured by desires for some forms of sociological or psychological satisfactions. As Taplin said: 'We spend most of our time not in keeping alive but in making life worth living.' (8)

Consumer wants are therefore partly tangible and partly intangible. Strictly informative advertising (were that possible) could tell the consumer whether or not the advertised product was capable of meeting the tangible wants. The consumer, however, also wants help in the purchase situation in deciding which of a range of alternatives will best satisfy his or her other and intangible wants. The advertiser can only help the consumer in this way if he moves away from objective lists of facts, and moves towards 'industrial poetry'. He cannot know precisely what motivates a woman to buy perfume, but he does know it is a result of a desire for glamour, romance and attractiveness. If so, how does he let the consumer know that his product can help provide such satisfactions? This he may do by using photographs of sophisticated women in smart social surroundings, or of a girl tête-à-tête with a good-looking partner over a dinner table.

These are situations in which perfume is used and are examples of satisfactions perfume buyers seek. Pictorial descriptions of such satisfactions are certainly persuasive. It would seem illogical, if these are the satisfactions which consumers seek, to condemn advertising which attempts to describe such satisfactions.

Such descriptions, of course, are no more the literal truth than expressionistic paintings are faithful reproductions of reality. Expressionism is 'the distortion of form and colour to aid emotional interpretation'. The persuasive aspects of advertising could similarly be defined as the selective dramatisation of selected product data to aid emotional choice.

That this, strictly speaking, is untruthful is no cause for condemnation. Provided one accepts the undesirability of human wants over and above subsistence level and provided that the 'selective dramatisation' is not dishonest and misleading, then a positive answer can be given to the question posed earlier in the discussion: Is or is not the use of emotional appeals desirable when the individual is in the purchase situation?

4. Does Advertising Make People Buy what They do not Really Need?
Once it is conceded that advertising is persuasive it follows that advertising is an influencer of consumer choice. The moral question is whether this influence is an aid to the making of a (relatively) free choice, or whether it is a distorter of choice? It is worth noting that in most cases uninfluenced choice is a practical impossibility. Uninfluenced choice requires the consumer to have full knowledge of the merits and demerits of every feasible alternative. Every first-year student of economics knows that perfect information of this sort is impossible. The only practical alternative is to provide arguments why people should try one particular product rather than another, and vice versa. Provided the consumer is free, firstly to agree with or ignore any particular set of persausive arguments, and secondly to choose any particular product in preference to another, there is little scope for condemnation of persausive advertising.

But does this influence of consumer choice not extend so

far that it makes people buy what they do not need? This question requires rephrasing. Modern society exists by producing goods which people do not need. People buy cars, not horses. They buy bungalows and semidetacheds, not tents. They buy high-fashion clothes, not animal hides. People's wants, both material and emotional, run far ahead of their basic needs for survival.

The question takes on a more serious air if it implies that manufacturers make consumers buy what they, the producers, want them to, and not what the consumers themselves really want. This is the stance taken, for example, by Packard. In *The Hidden Persuaders*, he writes:

> ... a good many of the people-manipulating activities of the persuaders raise profoundly disturbing questions about the kind of society they are seeking to build for us. Their ability to contact millions of us simultaneously ... gives them the power ... to do good or evil. (9)

This can be put more succinctly by asking if advertising *creates* the values of society, or whether is merely *reflects* them? Unfortunately this question is well-nigh impossible to answer. Probably the truth is that advertising can, and does, do both. Certainly advertisements influence consumers. Nevertheless it could be argued that if a product proves unsatisfactory it will not be purchased again, no matter how appealing is its advertising. In the final analysis, advertising can only sell goods which at least approach what the consumer 'really wants'.

Then again it could be argued that advertising encourages consumption of goods which in the short run the consumer 'wants' but which in the long term may be positively harmful. Cigarettes and alcohol are two commodities which spring to mind. Their association with cancer and cirrhosis is quite clearly alien to long-term consumer wants. Once more the question of want creation or want reflection is posed. Smoking, drinking and advertising probably have equally long genealogies in the history of mankind. Which arose first? Analogies are never wholly accurate, but it is tempting to point to the large increase in the incidence of drug taking throughout the Western World in the sixties and seventies. The taking of marijuana and harder drugs rose dramatically in this period, particularly in the younger age groups. How can the appearance of this global 'want' be explained? Whatever the answer it certainly owes nothing to advertising. Yet if marijuana production and consumption becomes legalised, there is no doubt that producers would commence to promote and point out the qualities of, and differences between their respective brands.

Equally, of course, advertising does help create wants or social mores which were not present before. But, unless such 'new' wants offend against generally accepted standards of behaviour, this is not a matter for condemnation. Changing and newly emerging wants are a sign of social progress, at least as measured by the normal indicator of economic growth. For example, all poor men want an adequate supply of bread to stave off hunger. With increasing wealth they would add the 'want' of meat, and ultimately, they would also add a variety of non-food wants. Advertising can help awaken or 'create' such latent or new wants in people. No one would 'want' colour TV unless, firstly, someone thought up the concept, and secondly, potential consumers were told that the concept had been translated into a piece of hardware available for purchase.

Some, of course, may question the validity of economic growth itself as a desirable goal, and hence, by implication, the part advertising plays in stimulating that growth. The abandonment of economic growth as a social goal, however, is almost if not wholly impossible. Growth depends on three main inputs: labour, capital and technological change. Zero population and zero net investment are feasible, if unlikely achievements. No country has yet attained zero population growth, although in advanced countries such growth has tended to flatten out in recent years. Zero net investment, even if desirable, would be difficult to achieve given a progressively rising propensity to save as disposable incomes increase. Of the three contributors to economic growth, technological change is the most important. (10) This variable cannot be rendered static as long as *homo sapiens* remains a thinking creature. As long as mankind continues to think, new products and new techniques of production will continue to raise productivity and lead to economic growth.

Even if this is conceded, however, opponents of economic growth may still argue that want proliferation, and any attendant advertising in the advanced countries is immoral. They might argue that economic resources should be redirected to improving the lot of the inhabitants of developing nations. They have a case. In this argument, however, advertising is neutral. Advertising can be used just as forcefully by organizations such as Oxfam, Christian Aid and Unicef as it can be used by a manufacturer of plastic gnomes.

Branding: A Digression
Brand names are the vehicles which link the advertisement to the product advertised. As a consequence many of the criticisms levelled at advertising are levelled also at the practice of branding. For example, Professor Boulding has written that 'most advertising, unfortunately, is devoted to an attempt to build up in the mind of the consumer irrational preferences for certain brands of goods . . . to persuade consumers that they should buy Bumpo rather than Bango'. (11)

This is simply a rephrasing of the charge that advertising makes people buy what producers want them to, and not what the consumers want themselves. Casual observation provides support for the charge. Consumers certainly become 'brand loyal'. Men often 'prefer' always to smoke the same brand of cigarettes. Women often 'choose' to use always the same brand of soap powder. Such loyalty may be the result of genuine or 'irrational' consumer preferences: which of the two views is seen as the more correct will depend largely on the stance of the observer.

On the other hand, it has already been argued that if a product provides inadequate satisfaction it will not be bought again, no matter how persuasive the advertising. The introduction of branding into the discussion strengthens this argument. If a product is unsatisfactory, a brand makes it readily identifiable, and so avoidable. An unsatisfactory brand will, other things equal, be withdrawn from the market more rapidly then a non-branded equivalent as a result of consumer resistance. The consumer will know which product to avoid.

Identification is the key advantage of branding. If a particular product is known to be satisfactory, then the consumer can be sure that he will receive the identical satisfaction next time he purchases it, irrespective of date or place of purchase. This implicit guarantee of consistency cannot be present with non-branded products. Professor Sir D. H. Robertson put forward this argument mundanely but succinctly when he suggested that 'there is . . . real spiritual comfort in buying a packet of a known and trusted brand of cocoa rather than a shovelful of brown powder of uncertain origin'. (12)

Branding coupled with advertising puts the responsibility for product quality on the shoulders of the manufacturer. It provides a strong economic incentive to ensure a consistent and high quality of output. If this incentive were absent the tendency could be for quality to suffer, and responsibility for quality might then have to be assumed by some outside agency such as a government department.

5. Does Advertising Hamper Freedom of Speech?

It is a fact that most national newspapers would have to be sold at a price several times greater than they are at present if they were to survive without the advertising revenue. Table 3.2

Table 3.2. *Advertising revenue and sales income of Newspapers and Periodicals, 1972*

	Sales (£m)	*Advertising (£m)*	*Advertising as % of total revenue*
Total newspapers	226	288	56
Sundays	46	39	46
Daily mornings	107	89	45
Daily evenings	55	95	63
Weeklies	18	63	78
Total periodicals	114	105	48
Trade, technical and professional	30	51	63
Other	84	54	39

Source: Business Monitor, (1973) 69—74.

shows how dependent is the press on advertising as a
source of income. Commercial TV is even more dependent on
advertising, receiving insignificant revenue from other
sources. The question is begged, does he who pays the piper
call the tune? Is our 'free press' less free in its ability to
express opinions than we like to think?
Without inside knowledge one can only speculate. Certainly there is scope for an unscrupulous advertiser to
threaten to withhold a campaign unless a newspaper editor
agrees in some way to use his paper's influence to aid the
advertiser's ends. Papers could conceivably be influenced in
this way either to withhold news items or to include editorial
material in line with the advertiser's desires. Furthermore
there is no reason why such influence should be restricted to
advertised products; it could also be used to further pet
political projects of the advertiser.
    This may or may not go on. Fortunately there are checks
and balances in the system which possibly minimise the risks
of such abuse. Firstly, while the advertising *industry* is a
major source of financial revenue for the media, any *one*
advertiser will be responsible for only a small fraction of total
revenue. Hence a threat to withhold a campaign is not so
powerful a weapon as it might at first appear.
    Secondly, all media editors thrive on newsworthy ex-
posures. Any advertiser who attempts to influence the
editorial policy runs the risk of having the attempt pub-
licised. The recent history of both the press and TV in Britain
provides little evidence of reluctance on their part to incur
the wrath of potential advertisers by reporting on poor-
quality products, substandard services or inadequate management.
    Thirdly, if an advertising medium provides good and
efficient coverage of an advertiser's target market, then that
advertiser cannot afford *not* to use the medium, irrespective
of its editorial content.
    Possibly then, freedom of speech is not impaired as might
be feared. Nonetheless it would be idle to pretend that the
danger does not exist.
    There is another view to the issue, which is that advertising
increases freedom of speech. For example, in a shrinking

world, more and more people are concerned about national and international issues. In this situation the soap-box orator is obsolete, the village meeting is redundant. To express views or concern about national matters one must use national media. Unless the views one wishes to express are newsworthy in themselves, the only way to obtain coverage in the national media is to buy advertising time or space. This is precisely what has been happening in many industrial relations disputes. Since the postmen first used advertisements to state their case during the 1971 postal strike, both employers and trade unions have frequently had recourse to newspaper advertising to tell the public why a dispute was necessary. (Rarely is this freedom denied. One denial, however, was during the 1972 rail dispute, when the Communist-controlled *Morning Star* refused to accept advertisements from the neutral Commission on Industrial Relations which contained information for the benefit of union members about the Government-ordered secret ballot.)

4 Decisions of Advertising Management

*Probably half of every advertising
appropriation is wasted,
but nobody knows which half.*

Lord Leverhulme

Advertising is suspected of being in excess of both its social
and commercial optimum level. Profit-maximising businessmen have no reason to carry the activity beyond the point
where the last pound spent on advertising brings in exactly
one pound more of net revenue. Yet the late Lord Leverhulme's statement suggests that they do exceed this point.
Why should this be? How do businessmen decide on their
advertising budget levels? How do they allocate their budget
among the various media available? This chapter is concerned
with providing answers to these questions.

1. Budget Determination
(a) Theoretical Models
Figure 4.1 shows graphically how sales and profits may vary
with advertising expenditure. Even with zero advertising,
some sales will be achieved by a firm. Little impact on sales is
made when advertising is indulged in at fairly low levels, since
the expenditure is so low as to pass unnoticed by the
majority of potential purchasers. After a point, however,
successive increments in advertising expenditure will produce
more than proportionate increments in sales. The sales-

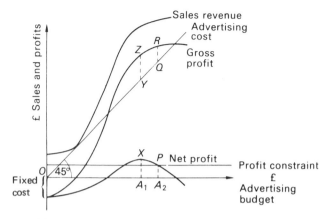

Fig. 4.1. *A model for determining the advertising budget*

revenue or response curve begins to rise steeply in Fig. 4.1. The firm has crossed the threshold level below which its advertising will pass unnoticed, and is reaching the stage where it can take advantage of economies of scale in advertising. Specialists in copywriting and design can be employed. Advertising research can be engaged in. More efficient media can be used. For example, a firm with £1000 to spend may be able to purchase for that sum one page in a paper with 10,000 readers, giving it a cost per contact of 10p. Such a firm would be precluded from taking a page in a five-million readership paper at a cost per page of £50,000, but an average cost per contact of only 1p. Eventually the sales-response curve will move out of this exponential phase, diminishing returns to advertising expenditure will set in, and while the curve will continue to rise, it will do so less than proportionately and, as a whole, will take on an S-shaped appearance. The diminishing returns will be due to fixity in size of the target market. Sales saturation will be approached; those customers most amenable to persuasion will already have bought, and only the less-willing prospects will remain.

Given that the two axes of Fig. 4.1 are drawn on the same scale, a 45° line can be drawn through the origin, and the vertical distance from any point on it to the *x*-axis can then usefully be represented as advertising cost. This equals the distance on the x-axis from where that intersection occurs to the origin. With knowledge of costs, other than advertising costs, for each sales level, the profit-curve gross of advertising expenditure can be drawn. The net profit curve can also be inserted. The boat-shaped area between the gross-profit curve and the 45° line equals net profits.

The profit-maximising firm will consequently produce at that sales level where net profits are maximised (XA_1), which is where advertising costs will equal YA_1 which equals a budget of OA_1. This model can readily be adapted to aid budget determination in firms with motives other than profit maximisation. Baumol, for example, has argued that firms maximise sales rather than profits. (1) Clearly, under this assumption, unless advertising became subject to negative or zero returns, it would pay businessmen to advertise until profits fell to some minimum acceptable level such as the profit constraint in Fig. 4.1. (Often, this is regarded as the minimum level of profits necessary to maintain share prices and dividends to shareholders at consistent or steadily rising levels.) In this case the firm's advertising budget would be set at OA_2.

This model, however, has several practical and theoretical disadvantages.

1. It assumes that advertising can be varied smoothly and continuously. In fact, this is not so. A campaign may be increased or decreased in extent, but this can only be done in discrete 'lumps'. One insertion more or less in a magazine campaign, for example, can represent an increase or decrease of several hundred pounds in expenditure.
2. It takes no account of the fact that sales vary with elements in the marketing mix other than advertising. They vary, for example, with price, choice of distribution channel, and product quality. Optimising all four elements in the mix may very well produce a different budget level from that when the other three are disregarded.
3. No account is taken, except in passing, of other costs, such as manufacturing costs.
4. It assumes that sales response functions *can* be con-

structed, that the relationship between advertising and sales is known with some exactitude. Unfortunately this is not the case.

5. No account is taken of the possible reactions of rivals to any selected advertising level.
6. The fact that advertising today can result in sales tomorrow, and that today's sales will to some extent depend on past advertising is ignored. It is a single-period model.
7. Advertising varies in quality, effectiveness and appeal, often in a manner unrelated to the level of advertising expenditure.

One other model which has been suggested takes several of these points into consideration. This is Verdoorn's model for determining the firm's optimal input mix. (2) It wholly overcomes objections 1, 2 and 3, and, at least partially, objection 6.

The basic model is shown in Fig. 4.2. Cost and gross revenue are plotted on the *y*-axis, quantity sold, on the *x*-axis. One particular selling price is selected. Price then

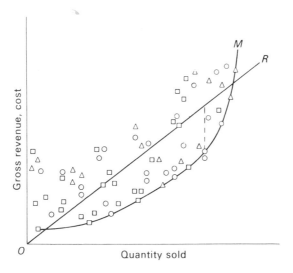

Fig. 4.2
Source: Verdoorn, op. cit.

being given, the total-revenue curve is a straight line passing through the origin, revenue varying directly with sales. Verdoorn examined three different product qualities, symbolised by a square, a circle and a triangle. The limitation to three is purely to prevent the graphical exposition becoming too complex. For each quality there will be a range of possible promotional outlay (including advertising) and distribution channel combinations. Thus selling through a wholesaler would require relatively high channel expenditures (discounts granted) *vis-à-vis* promotion, while selling direct would require low channel expenditures but the firm would have to undertake the expense of its own promotion. Selling through Marks and Spencers will require high discount levels but negligible advertising, since in this case the store itself undertakes the advertising effort of promoting the 'St Michael' brand. Conversely, selling through other retailers and using the manufacturer's own proprietary brand name requires much heavier advertising (and so possibly lower discount costs) in order to get the public to pull the brand through the channel.

For each quality, each practical promotion and channel combination is examined and costed. Advertising and promotion costs are aggregated, sales for the quality in question at the given price are forecasted, discounts and other channel costs are added to the cost figure, and finally, total cost is arrived at by including production costs for the estimated level of output. The total cost is then plotted on the graph against quantity sold, as in Fig. 4.2, using the appropriate symbol to identify the quality.

The minimum plotted points for any sales level, when joined together, provide a least-cost curve. The curve will obviously rise as more is produced. It will rise slowly at first as fixed costs are spread more and more thinly and as economies of scale set in. After a point it will rise more rapidly due to the advent of diminishing returns. Maximum profits will be earned at that point on the cost curve where the vertical distance between it and the total revenue line is greatest.

A series of similar diagrams can be drawn for a variety of prices, with different revenue *and* cost curves in each case.

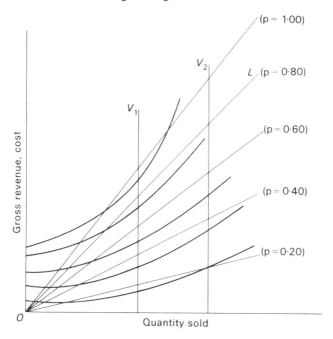

Fig. 4.3
Source: Verdoorn, op. cit.

(For any one output level production costs will not vary but, as price is raised or lowered, advertising and promotion costs will vary inversely. Furthermore, while percentage discounts granted may remain static, as price rises and falls, so too will the absolute level of discount granted.) The various price and cost line combinations can then be summarised on what Verdoorn calls a 'recapitulation diagram', as in Fig. 4.3. The overall point of maximum profit can then be readily found, and the appropriate choice made as to price, channel, product quality and advertising. Clearly, since only the plotted points on the diagram are practical possibilities, maximum profits will not simply be at the greatest vertical distance between any pair of cost and revenue lines. Rather, they will occur at that plotted point on the diagram closest to this hypothetical distance.

Thus the model overcomes the problem of discontinuities,

of sales varying not only with advertising but with the total marketing mix, and of failure to include production costs in the decision process. Finally, although it is essentially a single-period model, certain constraints can be added to it which enable the decision taker to take account of longer-term factors. The constraints are represented by the lines V_1, V_2 and L. The long-run profit maximiser will only choose an output level within the area bounded by these curves. L represents the highest acceptable selling price the businessman will charge. This constraint could be generated from fear of encouraging new entry into the industry which might, in turn, injure the prospects of long-run profitability. Or it could be set to avoid antagonising customers or to avoid drawing the attention of the Monopolies Commission to the firm. V_1 represents a level of output below which the firm will not produce. This could be the result of a refusal to pay off skilled labour who might prove difficult to re-engage. It could also be due to a desire to avoid disappointing or antagonising customers and losing goodwill by refusing to supply, or by supplying only at a discouragingly high price. V_2 represents the limit of expansion the businessman will consider. He may refuse to maximise short-run profit by producing beyond V_2 because, for example, such growth might lead to an expansion requiring an injection of outside equity, and so dilution of personal control. Or again, production beyond V_2 may lead to control of a level of market share which would induce examination by antimonopolies watchdogs.

(b) Practical Models
Verdoorn's model merely requires the application of numbers to the variables discussed in order to render it highly practical. Unfortunately, in most instances this is a well-nigh impossible requirement. To do so the decision taker must be able to predict the level of sales which will be attained with any advertising budget (at the stated price, the given product quality and through the chosen distribution channel). Even the experience of what the relationship between sales and advertising has been in the past is of limited value in predicting a sales-response function. £100 of advertising

expenditure next year may have a totally different impact on sales from that of £100 expenditure this year. Advertisement design or style will change and the qualitative impact of an advert often bears little relationship to the resources spent in creating it. Alternatively consumer preferences may change, either for the final product itself, or in the way they respond to advertisement styles. Competitors, who may have remained quiescent during this year's campaign may react vigorously, for example, by counter-advertising or price cutting, in future periods. What effect will that have on sales response? Furthermore, this year's advertising will have some sort of carry-over effect into next's. So the manager attempting to construct a predictive sales-response function must not only take into account the facts that advertising may differ qualitatively, and that rivals and consumers may react differently, he must also include in his calculations the fact that the 'goodwill input' at the commencement of each period will differ and will, in turn, alter the shape of the response function from one period to the next.

Faced with these problems many firms turn to less rigorous but more practical methods for setting their advertising budget. Four of the more common ones are described by Joel Dean. (3) These are:

(i) The percentage-of-sales approach.
(ii) All-you-can-afford approach.
(iii) Competitive-parity approach
(iv) Objective-and-task approach.

(i) The Percentage-of-Sales Approach
Ease of decision taking is a major advantage of this approach. The advertising budget is set at a level equal to some predetermined percentage of past or anticipated sales. The added attraction of apparent safety is present in that sales receipts and advertising outlays tend to coincide. However, no guide is given as to what percentage should be chosen and it seems probable that the 'dead hand of the past' will be a powerful influencer of choice. Firms will tend to choose that percentage which they traditionally use. Ideally, of course, the budget should be set in such a way that the outlay maximises the return from the resulting sales. There is

no reason why some arbitrary and consistent percentage of sales will achieve this aim. The approach rests on some other illogicalities also, particularly with regard to the sales base from which the budget is calculated. The use of future sales as the base from which to calculate the percentage has at least some rationale. (Although achieved sales will depend on many other factors as well as advertising expenditure.) The same cannot be said for the use of past sales. Advertising is meant to *cause* sales in the future, not be the *result* of sales in the past. Yet this is the implication when budgets are set at some percentage of past sales.

(ii)   The all-you-can-afford Approach
Here the firm spends on advertising up to the limits of its cash resources. The reasoning behind this approach bears a strong similarity to newer theories of the firm in micro-economics. Oliver Williamson, (4) for example, suggests that firms must meet some 'minimum profit' level in order to maintain expected shareholder earnings, equity prices in the stockmarket and to carry out essential investment expenditure for replacement or normal expansion purposes. Above this minimum level, however, management will spend corporate resources on factors which increase its own utility. In so far as each manager obtains utility from the number of staff personnel reporting to him (as Williamson suggests), since this reflects the individual manager's status and prestige, then managers will attempt to increase the size of the firm in order to increase, in turn, the size of their staff establishment. Clearly, one means of increasing firm size is to use those profits above the minimum level required on advertising.

   In practical terms this could mean that the advertising budget is set as the result of some sort of dialogue between the firm's financial and marketing directors. Certainly, one apparent advantage is that the approach sets a definite ceiling on what will be spent. The ceiling, of course, may be well above the profit-maximising level. Conversely, it is not inconceivable that the ceiling may be below the optimal level. Profitable market openings might be present in forthcoming periods for which past profit levels are insufficiently high to support an optimal advertising budget. In such cases the firm might be better advised to borrow resources for advertising, rather than be limited to 'what it could afford.'

(iii)   The Competitive-Parity Approach
This method again has the attraction of apparent security. The firm spends on advertising at the same percentage of sales, assets, market share or some other variable, as its competitors in the same industry. On the assumption that the relevant data can be obtained, the method has the advantage of simplicity. However, with the differing degrees and directions of corporate diversification, it seems unlikely that any one firm can identify itself completely with a group of firms all of whom are allegedly competing in precisely the same market. For example, a paint manufacturer mainly selling to the painting trade will require differing levels and styles of advertising from another firm selling primarily to the do-it-yourself market. Further, the first firm could be diversified in a small way into wallpaper production, the second might be operating in a wholly unrelated industry. Even if appropriate comparisons can be made, there is no reason why the budget selected should be optimal.

The method can also breed complacency, which could be rudely shattered if one aggressive firm decided to break ranks, and gained a substantial competitive advantage before sleepier rivals reacted. Similarly a smaller firm which unthinkingly followed the industry pattern might well find itself below a threshold level of advertising where its voice just could not be heard. Such a threshold is an absolute not a relative barrier. (Figure 7.4 indicates how small firms ignore this threshold at their peril.)

(iv)   The Objective-and-Task Approach
The previous three methods implied that allocation of the total budget by product, region and advertising medium *followed* the determination of the total budget. This approach tackles budget determination in the reverse order. The firm first defines the objectives it wants the advertising to attain. For example, an objective may be to achieve sales of product A in territory Z of some specified amount.

Secondly the advertising tasks which must be done to reach
that objective are defined. The programme could, for
example, take the form of a media campaign, say, six inserts
in the local paper serving territory Z in a specified period.
Finally, the tasks are costed, the costs aggregated and so the
budget obtained.

Up to a point, of course, this is only a slight advance over
the percentage-of-sales approach. Once again, the tasks to
attain a given objective will usually be defined in terms of
what it *apparently* took to attain some similar objective in
the past. Thus, in the example given, six inserts in the paper
serving territory Z will probably be chosen to attain the
specified sales of product A only because six inserts had
achieved that result in the preceding period. The question of
whether five or seven inserts would be more profitable than
six will probably not be asked, and if it were, the choice to
change from six might well be made more in hope than in
certainty. But, given the current state of knowledge (or lack
of it), this is rather an unfair criticism. Ideally the tasks to be
determined should be related to the objective to be attained,
and not to any recorded relationship between the two in past
periods. However, past relationships are very often the only
starting point from which to work, given the difficulties involved in predicting future sales response to future advertising.

One slight modification to this approach would, apart
from the practical constraints already mentioned, bring it
closer to the theoretical ideal of marginal equivalency of
revenues and costs. The relevant question is 'whether an
objective is worth pursuing in terms of the cost'. With this
considered in the approach then only the more profitable
objectives would be chosen, and the firm would be moving
towards attainment of a profit-maximising advertising
budget. The company would, of course, still be none the
wiser as to whether marginal increases or decreases in
expenditure on prescribed tasks would result in any particular objective becoming more or less profitable.

2. Media Selection
(a) The Theory
For any given advertising budget, the well-known principle of marginal equivalency states that it will be optimally

allocated between media when

$$\frac{\Delta S_1}{\Delta A_1} = \frac{\Delta S_2}{\Delta A_2} = \frac{\Delta S_3}{\Delta A_3} \cdots = \frac{\Delta S_n}{\Delta A_n}$$

where ΔS represents an increment in sales at a given price, resulting from an incremental advertising change, ΔA, in one particular medium, denoted by the appropriate subscript from the series 1, 2, 3, . . . n, where n represents the total number of available media.

This is so, since if the ratios are not equal, as in

$$\frac{\Delta S_1}{\Delta A_1} > \frac{\Delta S_2}{\Delta A_2}$$

then it would pay to remove some advertising effort from medium 2 and transfer it to medium 1. This may be more clearly understood if numbers are assigned. Consider that medium 1 is TV, and 2, newspapers. Consider that, in each, an extra showing or insert costs £100. Assume that spending an extra £100 on TV will bring in an extra £2000 sales, and similarly, in newspapers, an extra £100 will only produce an extra £1000 sales. Thus

$$\frac{2000}{100} > \frac{1000}{100}$$

With a fixed budget it would pay to switch £100 from newspaper to TV advertising. £1000 of sales would be forfeited through less advertising in the press, but £2000 would be gained through the higher level of TV advertising. A net gain of £1000 would result. Ultimately, of course, continuing to switch advertising in this way from the press to TV will produce diminishing returns to TV advertising. The ratio $\Delta S_1/\Delta A_1$ will fall. Conversely, spending less on the press will tend to raise the ratio $\Delta S_2/\Delta A_2$. When the two ratios are equal the budget is optimally allocated.

The same conclusion can be illustrated graphically with the economist's well-known tool of isoquant analysis. An isoquant is merely a line which joins up points of equal value. In the theory of production, isoquants join up points of equal output. Here we will use isoquants to join up points of equal sales response to advertising. Figure 4.4 shows an example of an isoquant map constructed for this purpose. For simplicity, we will assume that a 15-second TV advert costs the same (£1000) as a full-page press advert. This assumption does not affect the validity of the discussion in any way.

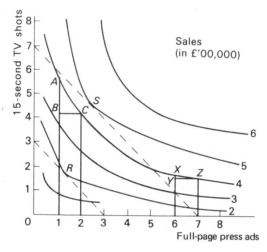

Fig. 4.4. *An isoquant map showing differences in sales response from differing media combinations*

Any sales-response isoquant which lies above and to the right of another has a higher value than that isoquant. This reflects the assumption that if expenditure on, say, TV is held steady, then an increase in press expenditure will result in an increased, not a decreased sales response. The isoquants slope down from left to right, reflecting the fact that if advertising in one medium is reduced, then to maintain an identical overall sales response, all other things equal, expenditure on the other medium must be increased.

Isoquant convexity to the origin is also assumed. This is a direct consequence of the assumption made earlier that there are diminishing returns to advertising expenditure, and that the respective sales-response curves are S-shaped for both media.* Consider two points on the same isoquant, A and X, in Fig. 4.4. At A, expenditure on TV is relatively high, and expenditure on the press is relatively low. At X the reverse holds. If diminishing returns to advertising expenditure do occur, then one would expect that at A, TV would be inefficient relative to the press as a medium, and relatively efficient at X. This, in fact, is so. If, at A, the firm decides to spend £1000 extra on press advertising, then to maintain constant sales the firm moves to point C on the isoquant and so saves expenditure on TV equal to the distance AB. At X, on the other hand, the press is relatively inefficient. Spending £1000 extra on the press and maintaining constant sales implies movement to point Z, a saving on TV expenditure of only XY.

Given knowledge of the firm's advertising budget, we can now include a budget line in the diagram. This can be defined as the locus of all combinations of TV advertising time and press advertising space which can be bought with a fixed budget. The broken lines represent alternative budgets of £3000 and £7000. On the assumption that the costs of the media to the firm do not vary with the amount spent, the budget lines will be straight lines.

The profit-maximising advertiser with a given budget will want to allocate the budget between the media in order to land on the highest possible sales response isoquant. With a budget of £7000, the media expenditure decision will be taken in order to arrive at the point of tangency, S, with the £500,000 sales-response line. Any other point on the budget line would intersect with a lower value isoquant. Similarly a £3000 budget would be allocated between press and TV to enable the firm to arrive at point R, the tangency point with the £200,000 isoquant.

Geometrically, at these points of tangency the slopes of the relevant budget lines and isoquants are identical. Thus, at R, the slope of the £200,000 isoquant equals the slope of the

---

*Technically, we are assuming that the marginal rate of substitution of TV for the press diminishes as more and more full-page press ads are substituted for 15-second TV shots.

£3000 budget-line sales isoquant; in other words,

any marginal increase in sales induced by a marginal change in TV advertising (dS_1)		any marginal increase in expenditure on TV (dA_1)
any marginal change in sales induced by a marginal change in press advertising (dS_2)	=	any marginal change in expenditure on the press (dA_2)

or

$$\frac{dS_1}{dS_2} = \frac{dA_1}{dA_2}$$

or in discrete rather than marginal terms

$$\frac{\Delta S_1}{\Delta S_2} = \frac{\Delta A_1}{\Delta A_2}$$

Dividing both sides by ΔA_1 and multiplying both sides by ΔS_2, we have

$$\frac{\Delta S_1}{\Delta A_1} = \frac{\Delta S_2}{\Delta A_2}$$

which is again the position of marginal equivalency.

Up to this juncture we have merely adapted the production function of the standard economics textbook for our own purposes. Now we must move beyond the normal stopping point of these expositions. The production function assumes a given technology. But technology embraces a variety of possible and known techniques. In real-life manufacturing there are always a variety of techniques open to the manager, not merely a variety of capital—labour input combinations. For example, the sources of supply for capital equipment are themselves diffuse. Thus items of machinery which are fundamentally similar often vary slightly one from the other in manner of use, quite apart from the range of labour inputs the manager can select to work each machine.

Similarly in real-life advertising there are always a variety of known message designs available for use, not merely a

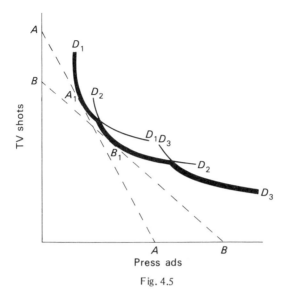

Fig. 4.5

variety of press—TV combinations using only one design type.

The typical graphical production-function isoquant is oversimplified. In order to take account of differing techniques of manufacturing, or in this case, differing message designs, some modifications are essential. In the area of general production theory Feller (5) has suggested the use of an arrangement of isoquants similar to that of Fig. 4.5. We will adapt this diagram specifically for marketing purposes. The isoquants represent the same level of sales response obtainable not only with differing media combinations, but also with different message designs. D_1, D_2 and D_3 represent three different design types. The thick 'envelope' isoquant, $D_1 D_3$, is the only isoquant relevant for the manager, since any part of an isoquant lying above the envelope curve would require at least more of one medium, and not less of the other medium, to produce a given sales level, than would be required by some other known, existing message design.*

*The isoquants in Fig. 4.4 are all implicitly 'envelope' isoquants for the relevant sales responses.

With a given budget line AA, the profit-maximising advertiser would select message design D_1, and would combine his media in the proportions indicated at the point of tangency A_1. If the costs of TV and press advertising altered, say, press became cheaper and TV more expensive, then the same budget could possibly buy the input combinations indicated by BB. Not only will media substitution take place as the advertiser moves to B_1 from A_1, but message design will also alter from D_1 to D_2. This analysis is not in the least inconsistent with reality. It is rather an attempt to bring theory closer to real life. If different manufacturing techniques can be embraced in Feller's modified production function, then so too can differing message designs. In the context of this discussion the two are analogous. Too often theory, both economic and marketing, neglects advertising creativity. Yet the sales effect of advertising is 'not simply a function of *how much* is spent. Even more important may be *how* it is spent.' Kotler subdivides the term creativity as referring first to what the advertiser says ('message content') and second to how he decides to say it ('message form'). (6)

Some flesh can now be put on the bones of Fig. 4.5 by means of the following highly simplified illustration. Consider an advertiser with problems of media selection and message design (content and form). The content decision could involve a choice, say, between a highly-descriptive advertisement with a lengthy exposition at one extreme, and a cryptic, abbreviated presentation of product-associated attributes at the other. The form decision could imply a choice, say, between a 'hard-sell' approach and a witty, playing down of the advertised product.

Thus, in Fig. 4.5, isoquant $D_1 D_1$ could represent varying combinations of press and TV advertisements which result in an equal sales response, given a message design D_1, which is a combination of minimum information and maximum wry wit. D_2 could represent a message design which is a combination of lengthy exposition and the 'hard sell'. D_3 could be the maximum humour plus maximum information, and so on.

Thus with a media cost line AA, message design D_1 would be chosen — minimum information, maximum wit — at media combination point A_1. This is not an implausible position. When TV is cheap relative to the press, as it is with cost line AA, then other things equal, TV will tend to be used relatively more by the advertiser than will the press. If this is so, then the message design which will be most effective will be that which is relatively most suited to TV, and least to the press. Conversely, when the press is cheap relative to TV, as with cost line BB, then media substitution will take place as indicated in the shift from A_1 to B_1. When such a movement is made towards buying relatively more press advertisements and fewer TV ones, then it should not be unexpected that a change in message design will occur, from one suitable to TV, to one more suited to the press.

D_2 is a more suitable message design than D_1 if the press is the economically more attractive medium, and vice versa.* Closely reasoned arguments require relatively large amounts of supporting information, and time for that information to be digested by the potential consumer. Newspapers provide the advertiser with the ability to put over large amounts of information and give the reader as long as he himself needs to assimilate it. TV adverts, on the other hand, are of necessity brief, and cannot be perused in depth at the discretion of the individual viewer.

D_1, however, is probably a more suitable message design when TV is the more economically attractive. Here TV will tend to be used relatively more than the press, and the strengths of TV can be exploited by the appropriate message design. Voluminous information is .precluded, but a lesser quantity of information may be all that is required, given the added impact of visual motion and aural stimulation. Moreover, if, as some have suggested, (7) people tend to be less willing to accept the credibility of advertising messages on TV than they do in the press, then it could be that the 'hard sell' will generate ill-will towards the advertiser, while a humourous approach might knit in better with the credulity

*Whether or not this is in fact so, may be open to dispute. Nonetheless, even if it were demonstrably incorrect, the validity of the argument would be unaltered. Only the appositeness of the illustrations is at risk.

attitudes people bring to their TV advertisement viewing
habits.

Innovation in Marketing

We can return here to the conventional theory of the
production function, at least for the purposes of graphical
analysis. A marketing innovation can be regarded as a change
in technology (as opposed to a change in technique). When
technological change occurs it is represented by the production-function surface taking on a new shape. The relevant
(envelope curve) isoquants move back towards the origin. In
the marketing context, we can say that the same sales
response can be achieved by spending less on advertising in
any one or both media.

This could be the consequence of any of several different
types of innovation in marketing. The introduction of colour
TV could make the advertising pound spent on TV more
effective. A totally new message design which had never
before been thought of could shift the isoquants towards the
origin. Increased knowledge of the target market, and more
sophisticated segmentation, could enable existing media and
known message designs to be combined more effectively than
before. The advent of perfumed paper, for example, could
well provide more sales per advertising pound in the press, if
and when, it became possible to select scents which enable
one advertisement to be distinguished from another.

As with the capital—labour production function of the
economics textbook, innovations in marketing can be classified in a manner akin to the Hicksian labour-saving, capital-
saving and neutral innovations of manufacturing. With given
media prices, marketing innovations can be classified according to their effect on the TV—press ratio utilised in the
achievement of a given sales response. Figure 4.6 illustrates
this. Each isoquant represents the same level of sales
response: *aa* is the original isoquant prior to innovation, *bb*,
cc and *dd* represent three alternative revised locations of that
isoquant, subsequent to three alternative innovations. Thus,
for example, the introduction and exploitation of a completely new channel of distribution could be regarded as a
marketing innovation. The growth of nationwide chains of
discount houses for electric household durables in the late

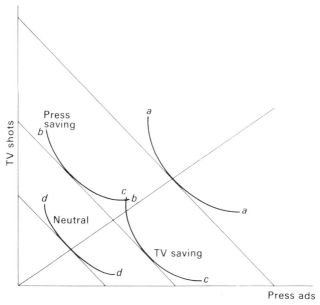

Fig. 4.6

sixties and early seventies is a case in point. Such an innovation may enable the advertiser to attain the same sales level with a lower budget than he otherwise could have with a more conventional distribution channel and price mix. Whether or not the innovation would be press saving, TV saving or neutral in its effect would, of course, depend on the individual case.

In the example cited, discount stores for electrical durables, it is a reasonable conjecture, if only from casual observation, that the innovation was TV saving. The press has become of paramount importance in this market, not only to announce the presence of a discount store in a locality, but to list in detail the range stocked, item by item and price by price. The absence of High Street window display makes such detailed advertising essential while, simultaneously, the detail involved renders TV relatively less efficient.

Thus, in allocating scarce budgeted resources, the advertiser, has three interdependent decisions to make. He has to

optimise media choice. He has to select the most effective
message design, and tailor it according to the media available.
(The media chosen, of course, will in turn depend on the
message types available.) Thirdly, decisions in both these
areas can be affected, and *almost always improved upon*, by a
successful marketing innovation. Conceptually it has been
shown how the economist's production function can help
pinpoint the profit-maximising solutions to these decision
problems.

(b) The Practice
It has been assumed throughout this discussion that the
response functions for press and TV advertising are independent one from the other. In fact they will interact. For
example, £1000 of press advertising in isolation may produce
10 units of sales. £1000 of TV advertising in isolation may be
equally effective. But if an advertiser spends £2000 and splits
it equally between the two media, the sales response may not be
10 + 10 = 20, but may be greater or less than 20. Synergy, a
greater total response than the sum of the individual responses
could come about if the strengths of one medium could be
transferred to the other, and vice versa. For example, a
person who normally ignores press advertising may be
encouraged to study a press advert in detail if he had seen the
same product advertised on TV the previous evening. *A
priori*, there is no reason why this complementarity may not
work in a negative direction also. In so far as the interaction
is positive it will increase the convexity of the isoquants, thus
a given budget line would be tangential to a higher isoquant
than it would be without the interaction. Conversely, if the
response functions react in a negative way, the isoquants will
tend to become less convex.

In so far as interdependent response functions are a more
accurate reflection of real life than independent ones, then
the principles of marginal equivalency as a means of media
allocation become even more difficult to put into practice.
As it is, the difficulties involved in predicting even independent response functions (see Section 1.b) force advertising
managers to turn to more pragmatic, less precise tools of
media planning. Managers will study the available media.

Media characteristics and suitability for promoting the product in question will be assessed. Media costs will be obtained, and a decision taken on the basis of whether or not the appropriate potential consumers are being reached at an acceptable level of expenditure. What are the various media available to a potential advertiser? The medium is the means by which the advertisement is conveyed to the market. Table 4.1 shows a breakdown of total British advertising expenditure by medium. In 1971 the single most important medium in terms of expenditure was TV, which accounted for 24.2 per cent of total expenditure. Newspapers, both regional and national, were however, only slightly less important than TV. And if the two groups of newspapers were counted as one, they would far outstrip TV in terms of expenditure levels with 44.0 per cent of the total. The characteristics of the media listed in Table 4.1 will now be examined in a little more detail.

Newspapers
The principal characteristic of the newspaper is its ubiquity. Everyone has access to the press, and almost everyone will read, or at least see, a newspaper each day. This enables the advertiser to get widespread coverage of his product instantaneously. The regular appearance of the daily papers can be argued to have two appealing features. They provide an obvious channel for repetition. And secondly, since readers are by definition looking for news, they may well be receptive to adverts for new products in the daily press.

If the regional press is used, the additional advantage of geographic flexibility is present. Advertisers can concentrate, according to choice, on areas where sales potential is highest, or on areas where turnover is slipping. Different advertising styles can be used in different areas, which enables regional or ethnic appeals to be included in the message. More prosaically, regional flexibility allows the advertiser to pass on localised information about place of sale, or regional price cutting. Comparative campaigns, using different styles and messages in similar, but separate regions is also a possibility with the regional press. Provided the test is well structured, and the test regions are alike in demographic and other

Table 4.1. *Total advertising expenditure by media*

Media	£m						% of Total					
	1960	*1967*	*1968*	*1969*	*1970*	*1971*	*1960*	*1967*	*1968*	*1969*	*1970*	*1971*
National Newspapers	64	84	99	111	108	108	19.8	18.3	19.7	20.4	19.5	18.3
Regional Newspapers	77	108	121	135	143	152	23.8	23.6	24.1	24.8	25.8	25.7
Magazines and Periodicals	40	46	50	53	51	54	12.4	10.0	9.9	9.7	9.2	9.1
Trade and Technical	31	43	46	50	53	52	9.6	9.4	9.1	9.2	9.6	8.8
Other publications	2	7	8	9	11	13	0.6	1.5	1.6	1.7	2.0	2.2
Press production costs	15	20	23	29	34	39	4.6	4.4	4.6	5.3	6.1	6.6
Total press	229	308	347	387	400	418	70.9	67.2	69.0	71.1	72.2	70.7
Television	72	124	129	129	125	143	22.3	27.1	25.6	23.7	22.6	24.2
Poster and Transport	16	18	20	21	22	23	5.0	3.9	4.0	3.9	4.0	3.9
Cinema	5	6	6	6	6	6	1.5	1.3	1.2	1.1	1.1	1.0
Radio	1	2	1	1	1	1	0.3	0.4	0.2	0.2	0.2	0.2
Total	323	458	503	544	554	591	100	100	100	100	100	100

Source: Advertising Quarterly, 32 (1972).

conditions, then the more successful advertising style can be chosen for wider use. (Subject to the additional *caveat* that the test areas are not dissimilar to the nation as a whole.)

The disadvantages of newspapers as a medium include the short lifespan which each issue has before it is discarded. The advertisement must share this transience. Secondly, the attention of the reader is not the monopoly of any one advertiser. Other advertisers, news coverage, photographs and editorials will all be competing for the reader's interest. Thirdly, despite the increasing use of colour inserts, colour is still uncommon in press advertising and when it is used is often poorly reproduced. Black and white photographs or sketches in newspapers also suffer from this defect of lack of clarity and sharpness. Clearly, poor reproduction is a major drawback when visual presentation of a product is of importance to potential buyers.

Magazines

Magazines fall into two main categories: consumer magazines and trade journals. Each accounts for approximately 9 per cent of total U.K. advertising expenditure. Both can be categorised by editorial approach. Every magazine has a viewpoint and style which attracts a certain type of reader which, in turn, enables the advertiser to select the type of audience most suitable for his purposes.

Consumer magazines can be subdivided into groupings such as general (e.g. *Reader's Digest*), women's (e.g. *Woman's Own*), fashion (e.g. *Vogue*) and special interest (e.g. *Autocar, Field, Practical Householder*). Trade journals can reach managers in industry generally (e.g. *Management Today*), or specific types of managers throughout industry (e.g. *Marketing, Accountant*), or all types of personnel in any one industry (e.g. *Textile Manufacturer, British Baker*).

Unlike newspapers, magazines are designed for leisurely, rather than hurried reading. Photographic reproduction, in both colour and black and white, is of a high standard. They tend to have a longer life than newspapers and may be perused over several days or weeks. (The typical dentist's waiting-room will inevitably contain an eighteen-month-old copy of *Punch*.) Some magazines may convey to the adverts they carry, and so to the products advertised, an implicit

stamp of social or quality approval. (In the late sixties, one
magazine used the following slogan to attract advertisers, 'Is
your product good enough to appear in the *Sunday Times
Magazine*?')

In the trade press, even more careful and informed study
of adverts by readers can be expected. There is also the
additional advantage that, with new products in particular,
editorial interest may be aroused, and so the product brought
to the readers' attention in a leading article.

The main disadvantage with magazines *vis-à-vis* newspapers
is that regional flexibility is lost, so message content must be
generalized to be meaningful to all readers. Local information
cannot be provided nor regional appeals used. (Although
some magazines with a global circulation, e.g. *Time* and *Life*,
do have editions which vary by continent of sale.)

Television

This is the single most important medium in Britain. It has
the obvious advantages of sight, sound and colour right in the
living-rooms of potential customers. The Independent TV
networks are regionally based, which enables the advertiser to
be geographically selective if he wishes. Flexibility by time of
presentation is also possible. The advertiser can aim at the
mass market between the hours of 8 and 10 in the evening;
he can aim at teenagers during the broadcast hours of pop
music programmes; or at men during the Saturday afternoon
sports shows.

The main disadvantages are the high absolute cost and the
need to get the message over in a few seconds. Costs can be
partially offset if a still display card rather than a moving film
is used, but probably only at the expense of effectiveness.
The difficulties of gaining the viewer's attention in competition with other adverts and the programmes themselves are
too well known to need repetition here.

Posters and Transport

Bill posters (or animated lights in the more populous areas)
and adverts inside and outside public transport vehicles are
seen by most people each day. This factor enables advertisers
to obtain the benefits of repetition cheaply and easily. The
major disadvantage is that people pass them swiftly, and so
the style and message must be such that it can be readily

assimilated. Geographic selectivity is possible with this medium, and the need for simple but direct messages means that it is highly suitable as a 'tie-in medium' to provide continuity with more detailed messages conveyed in advertisements elsewhere.

Cinema

The cinema has been steadily declining in importance as an advertising medium in the sixties. This possibly reflects the falling-off of cinema audiences as a whole. But it is possibly also indicative of neglect of the potential of the medium. It now accounts for barely 1 per cent of total U.K. advertising expenditure. Regional flexibility is present. Visual and colour reproduction is excellent and of a higher quality than is yet available on TV. Cinemas also have the advantage of being used by one opulent, but often neglected market segment, the new entrants, the teen and early-twenty age groupings who have yet to set up home and so become TV viewers rather than cinemagoers in their turn.

Radio

At 0.2 per cent of total expenditure, the radio (mainly Radio Luxembourg) is an insignificant medium in Britain. However, this situation will probably change dramatically with the spread of commercial radio over the next few years. The typical audience of Radio Luxembourg, homogeneous national youth, will not be replicated. Commercial radio will be regionalised rather than national. Inclusion of local current events programmes will ensure that the audience is drawn from the wider community.

The advent of this type of broadcasting may well attract others than just the big national advertisers. Local retailers, for example, will be able to get advertising shots broadcast over the appropriate network with less than one day's notice. The greengrocer with surplus stocks will be able to advertise price reductions in the morning and, hopefully, clear the shelves by the afternoon. At present, a greengrocer would have to wait, either for slow word-of-mouth communication getting around the town, or the local paper's weekly publishing day (probably already past), or he would regretfully be forced to accept deterioration of stock.

With knowledge of the media available and the budget to

be allocated, the manager must now select which media he will use. This will involve him in both an intermedia comparison (e.g. TV or press?) and an intramedia comparison (e.g. *Daily Mirror* or *Daily Express?*). The profit-maximising manager will want to reach as many potential customers as possible, to do so in the most effective manner and at the lowest practicable cost.

The charges which the various media set are readily available from the appropriate rate cards. (One well-known single source for newspapers and magazines is Maclean Hunter's *British Rate and Data*.) In newspapers and magazines the rate will vary with size of advert, use of colour, whether or not a preferred position is required, and whether or not the campaign will be a single shot, or will go on for a series of issues in the same publication — in which case quantity rates might well be quoted. Preferred position rates enable the advertiser to select, normally at a premium, the location of his advert. Some products may be more appropriately promoted on the women's page or on the sport's page of a newspaper than on a page selected at random. Advertisers of, say, fashion patterns and football boots might well be willing to pay such a premium for their 'preferred position'. Other common preferred positions are the inside and outside covers of magazines, sites next to editorial copy rather than competing advertisements, and so on. Similarly, TV charges vary with the time of day, day of the week, length of advert and use of colour. Time of day and day of the week are in turn associated with programme type and content, and so with audience nature. Once again the manager's task is to marry up his advertising with the desired audience in the most economical manner.

Media research data will tell the manager what sort and size of audience and what sort and number of readers will see his advert in any one medium. For example, circulation figures for newspapers and magazines can be obtained from bodies such as the Audit Bureau of Circulations. The major defect with circulation data, however, is that they only indicate the number of copies that have been sold. Obviously readership may be far greater than circulation, and there is no reason why readership figures will vary in the same proportions as circulation data for each paper or magazine. There are good reasons why the reverse may be true. The *Evening News* picked up from the station bookstall by a homeward-bound commuter may be discarded before he reaches his destination. Readership and circulation for that one copy are both equal to unity. The *Sunday Telegraph* delivered to that same individual's home at the weekend may be read by his entire family of four and by two friends who drop in casually for a visit. In this case, readership is six times greater than circulation.

As a result of the defectiveness of circulation data as a base for sensible decision taking, readership surveys have been developed. In Britain the most well known is the Joint Industry Committee for National Readership Surveys (JICNRS) carried out for the Institute of Practitioners in Advertising. This survey is carried out at regular intervals using a 30,000-strong sample of the total U.K. population. The objectives of the survey are to ascertain what numbers of the total population read which newspapers and magazines. Average readership per issue figures are then broken down by various demographic parameters such as sex, age grouping, income bracket, social standing and geographic distribution. (Such apparently esoteric information as ownership of lawnmovers and ordinary shares is also elicited. This data is of no little value to advertisers aiming at those customers with a strong interest in gardening or a high motivation and ability to utilise sophisticated savings media.) In sum, JICNRS data provides readership profiles, namely detailed statements of the characteristics of the readers of the various papers and magazines open to advertisers.

In like manner, viewership profiles can be obtained for TV audiences. The most well-known survey in the U.K. is the Joint Industry Committee's Television Audience Research (JICTAR) which is carried out on behalf of JICTAR by Audits of Great Britain Ltd. In essence, TV audience research involves attaching a mechanical recorder to the TV sets of a sample of the population. These recorders are checked weekly and indicate which sets were switched on, when, and to which channel. The basic defect with the mechanical recorder is that it does not tell how many people are watching the TV set, nor even if anybody is, in fact, in the room at the time. A diary lying alongside the set, which the viewer fills in on each occasion the set is used is a useful adjunct to the recorder. Data can be included in the diary about the nature of the audience in the house on each occasion. In aggregate, the various characteristics of the total sample can be extrapolated for the entire population, and viewership profiles for various programmes, days of the week, and times of day drawn up.

When readership and viewership profiles are known, the advertiser can then choose the medium, paper, magazine and/or time of day on TV which is most appropriate for his particular product. What is 'appropriate' will depend on who buys the product and/or who the advertiser would like to buy the product. In other words, the advertiser should have in mind, from customer knowledge gained from previous market research, a consumer profile, namely the groups of people most likely to be buyers, and their various characteristics. Advertisements, to be most cost effective should then be considered for placement only in those media where the buyer and readership/viewership profiles closely match.*

The decision taker's choice is still not wholly obvious, however. Few firms will have budgets large enough to advertise in each of the media with the relevant readership/ viewership profile. Other things equal, the medium with the lowest cost will be chosen. 'Cost' here will be relative not absolute. One paper, with a cost per page twice that of another, may have a readership four times as great. The relative cost comparison should not be the cost per page, but rather the cost per thousand readers.

Given equivalent costs and audience size, the advertiser may then select one paper rather than another, or one TV region rather than another, if comparatively more-attractive services to the advertiser are offered by that medium. Such services can include the circulation of all retailers in the

*More recently marketing and media data of this kind has been available from a single source. Since 1970 the British Market Research Bureau's Target Group Index (TGI) has provided detailed demographic information on the viewing and reading habits of purchasers of most non-durable consumer goods in the U.K.

region covered by the medium with proofs of the advertisement prior to its appearance. This encourages the retailers to have sufficient stocks on hand to meet the hoped-for increase in demand. Or the medium may offer before-and-after attitude surveys at special rates. 'Split runs' may be offered by some newspapers at little or no extra cost. This is the running of two or more different advertisement styles in the same issue of the newspaper. Thus if two styles are used, 50 per cent of the print will have one style, the remaining 50 per cent of the issue will contain the alternative advert. Some inducement, say a competition or a free offer, can be contained in the advert, to get customers to reply to it. Differently keyed addresses can be used in the two adverts, so that the advertisement style with the more effective response rate can be identified. Some media also offer advertisers attractive rates for the use of 'commando' sales teams. This is especially useful for new products or for firms entering a region for the first time. A team of salesmen, in addition to the firm's normal sales force, can be engaged for a short period to ensure maximum coverage of all retail outlets in as short a time as possible. Again the objective is to ensure that retailers' stock levels will be adequate to meet the demand induced by the forthcoming campaign.

With all these factors in mind — cost, services, audience size and type — the firm must finally examine the technical characteristics of the medium itself, and assess which is the most suitable for the product being promoted. Media characteristics have already been discussed in detail. Examples of the questions which firms must ask include, 'Does our product require visual demonstration?', 'Since our product is well known, should we concentrate on goodwill advertising?' If the answers to these questions are 'Yes', then in the first case, TV might be the most suitable medium, and in the second, magazines might well be better than short-lived daily newspapers for 'reminder'-type advertising.

Finally, the advertiser must balance that well-known trio of variables: reach, frequency and continuity.

Reach is the number of people an advert makes contact with. The larger the reach, the more people are contacted. Reach is greater if the firm uses STV, Granada and Yorkshire

TV, than if it uses STV alone. However, with a given budget, expanding the reach will diminish the frequency. Frequency is the degree to which an advert is repeated in the same medium. A meaningful impression may not be made if frequency is too low. Repetition is necessary since different people are making their purchasing decisions at different times. One advert may not be remembered by those taking their decisions sometime after that advert has appeared. Furthermore, a low frequency level may result in a firm's campaign being drowned by that of another firm with a much higher level of repetition. However, engaging in very frequent advertising within a given budget, will diminish continuity.

Continuity is the extent to which a firm continues the campaign over a long period. Given that other firms may encroach on one's market share if continuity is not maintained, then reminder or goodwill advertising should be engaged in, even if only at a low level, for defensive reasons.

5 Despair – or Hope for the Future?

The conceptual tools for improving the quality of management decision taking are available. Unfortunately, it appears from the previous chapter's discussion that decisions are taken, not optimally, but rather with a series of more or less sophisticated rules of thumb. This, of course, is inevitable until greater precision is obtainable in assessing the relationship between cause and effect, between advertising and its results. At present, as Table 5.1 indicates, there appears to be an inverse relationship between measurement of advertising achievement and the relevance of that achievement to corporate goals. Although advertisers may hope that there is a logical hierarchical movement by potential consumers from advertisement exposure to favourable attitude change to purchase, there is no proof that this is so. Nor, if it is so for some consumers, is it known what proportion of the total market these might represent.

This chapter will briefly examine each group of management tools named in the fourth column of Table 5.1. The chapter will conclude by suggesting how, if the two most precise groups of measurement tools are combined, a type of response function can be constructed, and as a result,

Table 5.1

Advertising effect on potential consumers	Relevance to business decisions	Ease of accurate measurability	Normal measurement tool
Exposure	Low	High	Circulation, readership or viewership data
Awareness attainment			Recall or recognition studies
Attitude change			Opinion and attitude surveys
Sales			Post hoc studies, test marketing and econometrics
Profits	High	Low	Post hoc studies

Source: D. B. Montgomery and G. L. Urban, *Management Science in Marketing* (Prentice-Hall, 1970). The fourth column was inserted by the present author.

advertising decisions be taken on a relatively rational basis of marginal equivalency.

1. Readership Data

It was pointed out in Chapter 4 that circulation figures were an inadequate foundation on which to base advertising investment decisions. Readership (or, in the case of TV, viewership) figures are a much more solid base. Unfortunately, even average readership is not helpful to most advertisers wishing to measure the extent of exposure to their campaign. Most campaigns have more than one 'shot' or insertion in the media. As a result, while average readership may give *some* idea of the reach of a one-shot campaign, it will prove to be inadequate both for measurement of reach and of frequency of exposure in a campaign with two or more shots. The need to assess frequency because of the value of repetition in advertising is too obvious to be repeated again here.

The term 'opportunity to see' (OTS) with regard to an advert means just that. Thus for a one-shot campaign in a journal with an average readership of 5000, the readership and OTS figures would be identical. However, in a con-

Table 5.2

Total population of women	Numbers and proportions having:				
20 million = 100%	Zero OTS	One OTS	Two OTSs	Three OTSs	Four OTSs
Case 1	12.5m = 62.5%	—	—	—	7.5m = 37.5%

tinuous campaign with two or more shots in the same medium, measuring the frequency with which OTSs occurs is not so simple, mainly because, although readership may be static over the course of the campaign, it is highly unlikely that the *composition* of that readership will be static.

For example, consider a campaign with four inserts in a women's weekly magazine, which has an average readership of 7.5 million. The total target population is all women in the country, say 20 million. Assume the same 7.5 million read the magazine faithfully week by week, and the other 12.5 million never see it. Then, the situation in Table 5.2 exists. This is a very unlikely distribution of OTSs. In reality, some women will subscribe to the publication faithfully week by week, others will see it frequently but not consistently, while still others will be only spasmodic readers, buying the magazine on impulse or perusing it lightly in dentists' waiting-rooms and the like. Furthermore some journals will have a more loyal readership than others.

The results that this might have on the frequency distribution of OTSs throughout the target population are illustrated in Table 5.3.

Table 5.3

Members of Total Population with:	Zero OTS	One OTS	Two OTSs	Three OTSs	Four OTSs
Journals with identical average readership of 7.5m					
Case 2: High readership loyalty	50%	5%	10%	15%	20%
Case 3: Low readership loyalty	40%	20%	20%	10%	10%

In all three cases illustrated in the tables, the total readership potential is 4 x 7.5 million = 30 million readers. But, in fact, in case 1, only 7.5 million read the magazine, albeit on four consecutive occasions. In case 2, 10 million people saw the magazine at least once, but only 4 million saw it four times, while in case 3, 12 million saw it at least once, but only 2 million four times. Clearly the advertiser with a run of adverts in a medium is interested in this sort of data, the total and distribution of OTSs throughout the population, and not merely readership.*

Unfortunately, while OTSs are a more precise measure of the extent and nature of exposure to adverts, it does not necessarily imply that the OTS actually equals an opportunity taken, that the advert was in fact seen. This flaw will be examined in more detail in Section 5 below. The other defect, of course, is the lack of any proven relationship between OTSs and sales.

2. Recognition and Recall Studies
Readership and OTS assessment can be done on either a *post hoc* or *ante hoc* basis. Recognition and recall studies are essentially measures of effectiveness carried out *after* the advert has appeared.

(a) Recognition Tests
Recognition tests originated in the U.S.A. and were first described in detail in Dr Daniel Starch's *Principles of Advertising*. (1) Starch's main thesis was the simple one that

*The necessary information to construct tables such as 5.2 and 5.3 can be obtained from the answers to the National Readership Survey's questions on 'numbers of issues read or looked at' in a specific period. The period referred to by the NRS questionnaire is usually six days in the case of daily papers, and one month in the case of weekly publications.

Although this section has concentrated on illustrating how readership data can be converted to the more meaningful OTS there is no reason why viewership data cannot also be so converted. To do so would require using the diary-linked research programme in those sample houses already possessing the mechanical recorder attached to the TV set. The diary would be used to record which specific individuals had been watching the TV at the times the set was turned on. (Without a diary back-up the recorder merely gives data on numbers of sets switched on.)

the mere existence of an advert in a medium did not mean readers had seen it, far less assimilated its message. To counter this defect in knowledge about advertising's effectiveness he evolved the recognition test. In the U.S.A., Daniel Starch and Staff is now one of the largest organisations carrying out this type of advertising research. In the U.K., similar work is done by the Gallup Field and Readership Index of the Gallup Poll organisation.

Typically the system involves interviewing readers of the publication to be tested. The sample of interviewees is asked, for each relevant advert, if they had 'noted' it (i.e. remembered seeing it), if they had 'seen and associated' the advert with the product or firm in question, and finally, if they had 'read most' (i.e. more than 50 per cent) of the written material. After only a short time lag for processing the data, often as short as a month, the research house will come up with the scores for each relevant advert in each publication surveyed in the previous period. (For example, one of the most 'successful' adverts in Britain in 1970, according to the Gallup service, was for a Volkswagen 'beetle' in the 18 February issue of the *Daily Telegraph*, 84 per cent of all males adult readers having 'noted' it.) (2)

Advertisers can very promptly examine their scores, compare them with previous scores, with scores attained in different publications or different sites in publications, with scores attained with differing uses of colour, design or advert size and, of course, with scores attained by competitors' advertising similar products. Clearly this sort of information could be invaluable to decision takers, either as it stands, or, as is often the case, when the research house, with knowledge of both readership and the cost of insertion, converts its data into 'readers per pound' who have noted the advert.

Even with a well-designed sample and a good interview technique there are a number of limitations with the method. Not least, the implicit assumption that awareness of an advert leads to purchase. More specifically the scores may well tend to be exaggerated. Principally this will be due to false assumptions that the advert was in fact seen, for example, because the interviewee confuses the advert with a similar but different one in a previous stage of the campaign, but has in reality only noted the earlier one. Alternatively the interviewee may genuinely recognise material in the publication surrounding the advert, leading to a positive, but possibly false response. Finally, there is the normal human failing of wishing to please or impress the interviewer by appearing knowledgeable and well read.

(b) Recall Tests
These are less liable to provoke false responses by interviewees. The sample used is again based on actual readers of the publication being tested. But the respondent is not shown the adverts, as in recognition tests. Rather, he is asked to recall and describe the adverts he remembers seeing. There is little opportunity to exaggerate claims, and what is remembered is taken as an indication of high awareness attainment by the advert. This is unaided recall. In aided recall the interviewer may prompt the respondent by asking which product or firm types he remembers seeing advertisements for, and then asking him to describe these in more detail, hoping for mention of brand or company names, style or subject of advert, and so on.

Unfortunately the residue of people who remember well (in either the aided or unaided situation) may be very small and non-representative. So this type of testing may suffer from deflation of evidence as opposed to the possible exaggeration in recognition tests.

3. Attitude Surveys
(a) Pre-testing
Because people are generally very willing to cooperate when asked to assist in interviews, opinion surveys of adverts *before* they are inserted in the media are very easy to carry out in principle. Generally a sample is chosen, which can range in size from half-a-dozen girls in the typing pool to over a thousand people who are sent mailed questionnaires. The sample is asked what they think of the intended advert, how interesting and how credible it appears, what their reactions to it are and whether they would buy on the strength of it. This information can be elicited in a variety of ways, from individual interviews to group discussions, to asking the

respondents to rank a series of alternative adverts in order of merit. One major disadvantage lies in the very willingness of the sample itself to be helpful. The respondents may give their opinions as experts, as to how they think the public will react to the advert, rather than how they themselves would react. Whatever else the sample may be, it will *not* be composed of such 'experts', and so the opinions obtained may well not be those of the sample, *qua* sample of consumers. This sort of difficulty poses complicated psychological and methodological problems, and agencies will usually use skilled psychologists to construct the studies, guide the group interviews and interpret the results.

Another technique used to pre-test adverts, is the use of a mechanical device known as the tachistoscope. This is an instrument which has been used for many years by applied psychologists. Basically it flashes visual messages in front of the subject for controlled exposure periods. By questioning the subject after flashing the message for varying periods of time the researcher can discover which message type or style conveys its meaning to the subject most quickly.

Finally, there is the pre-testing of TV commercials. The most well-known technique in this field is that evolved by the Schwerin Research Corporation in the U.S.A. A consumer-jury sample is invited to attend a theatre showing of TV films interspersed with commercials. Each sample member is asked beforehand which of several brands he would prefer to receive a supply of if successful in a lottery. After the showing the same basic questions are asked again and any attitudinal change is duly recorded. Other competing techniques in this area involve for example, giving buzzers and bells to the audience. The buzzer is pressed if the viewer does not like the advert, the bell if he does, if he presses neither he is assumed to be indifferent to what he is seeing.

(b) Post-testing
Consumer surveys of attitudes to specific brands, taken before and after a particular campaign, are the commonest method of testing for attitude changes after the advert. Techniques can range, among others, from the simple questionnaire interview to the rather more satisfactory one of

asking the interviewee to place his evaluation of the brand along a seven-point scale of paired opposites. The number of such paired polar adjectives assessed will depend on the nature and extent of information required. This is the semantic differential technique. (3) It has several advantages over the normal interview. For example, problems of questionnaire construction, such as innuendo and ambiguity, are avoided. Response by the less articulate is facilitated, and the replies obtained are readily subject to quantification.

More profound information on attitudes can be obtained by the use of other motivation research tools such as projective techniques or depth interviewing. However, these must generally be confined to a small sample, and as a result, replication to obtain information on attitude *changes* may suffer from non-comparability of samples unless the same individuals are used on both occasions. This can also result in atypical information being derived.

The main advantage of measuring advertising effectiveness by attitude change is that a favourable change is presumed to be much more likely to result in a purchase than merely exposure to or memory of an advert. Whether or not this is so, and whether or not what is measured by the techniques are the relevant 'attitudes', can of course be matters of some debate. (4)

4. *Post-hoc* **Sales Studies**
Examining sales figures on a before-and-after basis is *prima facie* the most obvious way of assessing the effects of an advert. Unfortunately, the answer is almost as certain to be wrong as it is easy to obtain. Many other variables will have had an impact on sales in the period examined. For example, other elements in the marketing mix may have altered, competitors' activities and/or peoples' tastes may have changed. Further, the time factor will be unaccounted for in such a naive comparison. Sales achieved may well owe something to previous adverts, and the current advert may have considerable impact on sales in periods subsequent to that under examination. Furthermore the quality or appeal of an advert will also vary with the design of the copy. Rarely will similar expenditures result in identically attractive copy.

There are, however, three areas where sales tests of this sort may not be wholly misleading. These are direct mail advertising, test-market experimentation and econometric studies.

The actual response in terms of returned reply coupons taken from either circulars or newspaper adverts can only come directly from the advertising itself, not from any other part of the promotional mix. Even here, of course, other variables may also have impinged indirectly on the decision to return the coupon.

Secondly, if two differing geographic test areas are chosen which are identical in almost every respect except in the extent or style of one particular advertising campaign, then presumably, any sales differences which occur in those areas can be attributed to the advertising variations. In practice it is not always easy to select two such areas. The breakdown and nature of distribution channels, of social and demographic features, of competitive rivalry, of exposure to previous campaigns and of media readership and viewership must all be similar, otherwise experimental validity is forfeited.

One very interesting before-and-after study using a test-market area was carried out by Morris to evaluate the effects of a campaign sponsored by the Ministry of Transport, not to increase sales, but to increase usage of seat belts by car drivers and passengers. (5) The campaign took place in the late summer of 1971 in the area covered by Tyne-Tees TV (the test area). About 7000 cars were stopped and observed in the test area, and 8000 in the rest of the country (the control area), both before and after the campaign. Driver usage of seat belts rose from 14 per cent before the campaign in the test area, to 29 per cent after the campaign. This compared with a rise from 16 to 18 per cent in the rest of the country. The corresponding figures for front-seat passengers were 14 to 27 per cent in the test area and 18 to 21 per cent in the control area. Whether or not 'decay' set in after the campaign is not known, nonetheless seat-belt usage almost doubled during it, and this must largely have been due to the success of the advertising.

At least three writers have been successful in using econometric analysis in assessing advertising's effects, two working in America and one in Europe. Palda examined sales and advertising figures for Pinkham's 'Vegetable Compound' between 1908 and 1960, (6) Telser examined the three largest cigarette brands between 1912 and 1939, (7) (these included 'Lucky Strikes' and 'Camels'), and Lambin used twenty years' past data relating to an unspecified consumer non-durable to calculate the following statistically significant regression equation: (8)

$$Q_t = f(y_t, w_t, s_t, \Delta d_t, \Delta p_t, Q_{t-1})$$

where Q_t = sales in year t per 1000 potential customers;
   y_t = real private disposable income per 1000 potential consumers;
   w_t = weather conditions, rainfalls adjusted for seasonal variation;
   s_t = advertising expenditure per 1000 potential consumers;
   Δd_t = change in sales-force visit frequency to sales outlets;
   Δp_t = change in average retail price of the item;
   Q_{t-1} = A 'goodwill' variable to take account of the time element of advertising effects based on lagged sales data.

   Lambin admitted that he had not taken quality of advertising into account, but suggested that this had been fairly constant due to a similarity of style used by the same agency over the entire period. The state of competition was also omitted but, for the product in question, the author argued that the market was similar to a monopolistically competitive situation. Although many rivals existed, the cross-elasticity of demand was low, and the competitive structure had remained fairly static during the period of the study.
   The value of this sort of exercise is not limited to assessing in retrospect the part which advertising has played in sales change. It can, by providing a basic estimating equation, render it possible for businessmen to predict what effect advertising changes *in the future* will have on sales. In Lambin's example, if each independent variable could be

predicted (weather could be given an average value), then by substitution one could predict the different sales levels resulting from varying advertising budgets.

5. Response Functions *can* be constructed

Given production and other cost data for the various levels of output predicted for different advertising outlays in such an equation, a businessman could reach a decision on profit-maximising behaviour in the way suggested by Verdoorn's model of Chapter 4. Unfortunately most practitioners may be unable to use econometric analysis in this way. Estimating a sales-response function from a regression equation is attractively, and possibly deceptively simple. In most situations there will be variables which should be included in the study, but which defy quantification. (Happy is the researcher who, like Lambin, can say that advertising quality has remained constant for twenty years!) Furthermore there are many statistical and economic pitfalls involved in this sort of empirical demand estimation exercise, which even the most skilled can fall into, but which, if ignored, can result in downright misleading conclusions. (Simultaneous equation problems, identification difficulties, least-squares bias and multicollinearity are only some of the problem areas which may be encountered.) Baumol (9) and Quandt (10) have both written extensively on this subject and are worth consulting by those interested in probing more deeply.

Sales-response functions, then, can be constructed with econometric tools using *post hoc* data. Unfortunately this technique cannot assist in the construction of a response function for the total budget when past data does not exist. And second, it would be difficult to use in designing functions for each medium to assist in media allocation decisions. This is not an easy task whether or not past data exists, since in combined media campaigns it may be very difficult to assess in retrospect what proportion of total effectiveness should be attributed to each of the media. One way of overcoming this obstacle is to make *ex ante* predictions of the response function for each medium.

One of the most interesting and practical ways of constructing such response functions was described by

Corlett, (11) who constructed his response function by employing an ingenious combination of OTS data and noting scores. (As such, of course, the term 'sales'-response function is inappropriate, rather, the function calculated is of advertising effectiveness as gauged by these two tools, and so is open to the criticisms already levelled at them earlier in this chapter.)

The technique involves first calculating the average noting score obtained in the particular publication in some past period by adverts similar in size, style, colour, position, etc. to the one the firm is considering inserting. This average of these noting scores is then taken as the probability that such an advert's OTS potential will or will not be transformed into 'opportunities taken'.

Consider an advert with a predicted noting score of 50 per cent. A prediction of the response function for a four-insertion campaign in the woman's magazine described as case 2 in Table 5.3 is required. The first step is demonstrated in Table 5.4 which indicates how the OTS distribution is converted into the more relevant distribution of opportunities taken, or in different language, of advert exposures actually received by readers. By the normal theory of probability, half of those having one OTS will see the advert, and half will not. Similarly, of those having two OTSs, one-half will see it once,

Table 5.4

	All housewives	Members of population with:				
		Zero OTS	One OTS	Two OTSs	Three OTSs	Four OTSs
	100%	50%	5%	10%	15%	20%
Estimate of opportunities taken (advert exposures received)						
0	58.12%	50%	2.5%	2.5%	1.87%	1.25%
1	18.13%	–	2.5	5	5.63	5
2	15.63%	–	–	2.5	5.63	7.5
3	6.87%	–	–	–	1.87	5
4	1.25%	–	–	–	–	1.25

one-quarter twice and one-quarter not at all, and so on for the higher values of OTSs.

The conversion of an OTS frequency distribution to one indicating the extent to which such opportunities might, in fact, be taken removes one of the main defects of readership data. The degree to which such data can be misleading without such modifications is clearly illustrated by comparing, respectively, the first row and column of Table 5.4. (For example, while 20 per cent of the total population had four OTSs, only 1.25 per cent of the population actually took all of these opportunities and would have been exposed to the adverts.) Similar frequency-distribution conversions could, of course, be performed with average noting scores different from the 50 per cent used here.

The next stage is to 'specify the response function' from the 'advert exposures received' figures. This is done by assigning values to the different numbers of exposures. Manifestly the 15.63 per cent of the total population in Table 5.3 who receive two exposures will be more affected by the advertising than the 18.13 per cent who receive only one exposure. To transform each exposure datum to an appropriate effectiveness equivalent or response value requires modifying it by an appropriate weight. The weights should reflect the S-shaped sales-response function of Chapter 4, thus taking into account increasing, then ultimately decreasing, returns in advertising effectiveness.

Table 5.5 shows how a responsive function can be specified using arbitrary weights* to transform the advert exposure data of Table 5.4.

Column 4, marginal-response values, can be compared with the marginal sales achieved with given marginal changes in advertising outlay, referred to at the beginning of Chapter 4.2a. Each value refers only to that incremental proportion

---

*For illustrative purposes it has been assumed that for a four-insert campaign increasing returns to advertising inserts has been succeeded by diminishing effectiveness. Clearly the use of the *entire* length of the S-shaped function to base weights on in this way may not be valid until many more inserts have been made. This can only be judged on the merits of the case. It is possible, for example, that a pattern such as 0.1, 0.6, 0.8, 1.0 would have been more appropriate here (increasing followed by constant returns).

Table 5.5

1	2	3	4	5
Advert exposures	Relative effect-ness of exposures (arbitrary weights)	% Target group reached	Marginal response value 2 x 3	Cumulative response values
0	0	58.12	0	0
1	0.1	18.13	1.813	1.813
2	0.4	15.63	6.252	8.065
3	0.8	6.87	5.496	13.561
4	1.0	1.25	1.25	14.781

of the population effectively reached by one more or one less exposure. The cumulative-response values are then easily calculated from the marginal data. The cumulative data can be compared with the S-shaped sales-responsive function of Fig. 4.1. Intermedia comparisons and decisions can then be effectively made on lines very similar to those suggested by the marginal-equivalency formula of Chapter 4. The disadvantages of using arbitrary weights will be partially neutralised for comparison exercises of this sort if an identical system of weighting is used for calculating each medium's response function. Furthermore it is highly probable that assigning weights in this manner provides more realistic information for decision takers than not doing so at all. Failure to do so implies constant returns to advertising exposure, a most unlikely situation.

Reality is far more complicated than the last page or two has seemed to imply. Campaigns will normally have far more than four insertions. Not only must media be compared one with the other, but different patterns of media combination must also be considered. However, the difference in complexity which the practitioner would encounter is not so much of principle but of data collection and processing. Given the availability of computers, the construction of 'effectiveness' response functions becomes a feasible proposition.

None of the tools for measuring advertising effectiveness is perfect. All have major practical and/or theoretical drawbacks which preclude either practicability or accuracy or both. Given past progress, however, only fainthearts will deem it unlikely that greater accuracy can be attained in the future. If more satisfactory measures of advertising's effects are obtained then there will be a greater ability to predict what effects will be attained with what expenditure. In turn, more rational judgements by managers about whether an item of expenditure is, or is not, worth while can then be expected. Several existing methods of assessing advertising's effectiveness were mentioned earlier. In particular the econometric approach to constructing a sales-response function to total advertising expenditure was described, and in more detail, the means of attaining an 'effectiveness'-response function for each medium was examined.

Tools such as these need to be tried, tested and improved upon in practice. The more they can be refined in use, the easier it will become for managers to spend on advertising up to, but not beyond, the level where the extra revenue gained from the activity will equal its marginal cost.

6 Conditions affecting the Demand for Advertising

The purpose of Chapters 6 and 7 is to examine the various conditions affecting, respectively, the demand and the supply of advertising. This chapter begins by discussing what is unusual about the market in advertising. Next a possible meaning of supply and demand equilibrium in that market is presented. The remainder of the chapter examines how a variety of factors associated with either the characteristics of the consumer or of the product can affect the nature and intensity of the demand for advertising. In conclusion the question is posed as to whether more advertising is consumed or demanded than is economically optimal.

1. The Market in Advertising

Like all markets, the market in advertising can lay claim to being unique and so merit special analysis. True or false, it can certainly lay claim, for at least three reasons, to being unusual.

First, advertising can be partly regarded as a subset of the generic commodity information, or knowledge. As such, it is a 'public good'. A pool of information possessed by A can be utilised by B, and A will be no poorer as the result of that use. Consequently, advertising can only be 'sold' in the normal manner to a series of individual buyers if each pledges himself to join a syndicate of secrecy with the seller. Even if this were achieved, human nature would quickly render such a system worthless, and information would seep out to non-syndicated consumers.

Second, and as a direct result of the first point, advertising is normally jointly supplied with the product it promotes. In other words, the buyer must pay for both the product and the advertising, even if only the product itself is wanted. Product price will include a component to help recover advertising cost. Had advertising not been developed, then some other system would have been necessary to recoup the costs of distribution of product knowledge to potential buyers.*

Third, there is no one market in advertising; rather, the markets in advertising are legion. Supply and demand for any particular piece of product information is intimately, although not exclusively,† associated with the buyer—seller relations in the appropriate product market (for goods or services). There is a whole host of such product markets and axiomatically a similar number of markets or submarkets in advertising.

2. What is the Quantity of Advertising?

The advertising market is, therefore, if not unique, then certainly a very interesting subject of study. The economist examining the market is further challenged in that his conventional tools, the demand and supply curves of simple price equilibrium analysis, are not wholly adequate for his purposes.

---

*Discussion of alternative means of information dissemination is delayed until Chapter 8.

†Where product markets are closely related in terms of a high demand cross-elasticity due to the presence of close substitutes or completments, then, *a priori*, the demand for advertising in each of these markets will also be interdependent.

Motor car advertisements, for example, are of little interest to the buyer of margarine. Butter advertisements, however, are. Here the buyer would wish to compare prices, location of supply and other data before purchase of one or the other.

The normal price—quantity plane on which supply and demand curves are drawn implies that 'quantity' has only one meaning, increases or decreases merely representing more or less of some commodity which can be measured by homogeneous units. With advertising, this type of quantity change could be called a change in advertising *intensity*. Intensity varies when there are alterations in any of the trio of variables which practitioners call the 'reach, frequency and continuity' of a campaign. (For example, advertising in two TV networks instead of one, changing from a twice-weekly to a once-nightly showing and terminating a campaign after two months rather than one.)

But advertising cannot always be divided into homogeneous units; quantity changes can also occur when the *extent of the data variety* alters in an advertising campaign. For example, the information provided in an advert can range from the blunt '2p off' sign outside a garage, to the one-page or more of fine print contained in an Offer for Sale and Prospectus of newly issued shares. Collecting, processing and presenting a wide variety of data, is, *ceteris paribus*, a costlier job than doing so for a narrow range of data.

The analyst of advertising quantity faces yet another problem. The quantity of advertising (as measured by the common denominator of expenditure incurred) will also vary with the *style of data presentation*. This can range from the austere to the lavish; from small adverts to large; from the rational to the emotional. The style chosen will influence the quantity of advertising and the resources expended on advertising in no less a way than will the two other dimensions of quantity—intensity and data variety. For example, a 10-second TV shot which uses only a display card and the voice of an announcer will cost considerably less to produce than a similarly placed and timed shot which uses well-known actors and casts them in a mini-drama to convey the same basic data to the viewer. The increased quantity of advertising in this example is due to the higher costs of the changed advertisement style.

Even at a more objective level, the quantity of advertising can vary with style. No information is costless, either to transmit or to acquire for transmission. Thus it is cheaper for an airbed manufacturer to promote his products as 'able to stand up to hard wear' than to give the precise poundage of pressure per square inch required before the bed will burst. The outlay required will not differ because the intensity of advertising is changed, nor because the extent of data variety is altered. The press space required to print the numerical information will be little different from that required for the descriptive phrase: the data variety, the information conveyed, is essentially the same. But the manufacturer will have had to incur expense on relatively costly and precise product testing to obtain the numerical data (i.e. to alter the information style) for his advertisement.

3. A Conceptual Approach to Equilibrium in the Advertising Market

Given the many-sided nature of the 'quantity' of advertising, some modification to normal supply—demand analysis must be made. Before doing so it is worth asking what the equilibrium position would be in the idealised situation of perfect competition.

Under conditions of perfect competition, there is no demand for advertising. There is perfect and freely available information on price. Products are homogeneous, and given that producers are charging the market price, buyers are indifferent to which source they use. What has been called 'random pairing' between buyer and seller will be in operation. (1)

This is a useful starting point but it is universally regarded as an abstraction which bears little resemblance to real-life marketing. Products, conditions of sale, customers and suppliers are each heterogeneous groupings. Sellers are not indifferent to whom they sell. Buyers are not indifferent to whose product they purchase. So random pairing is not a realistic concept in a world of differentiated products and varying consumer preferences. Clearing the market, exactly matching the demand and supply of all available goods and services (which is the object of all marketing), is no longer a matter of merely arriving at an equilibrium price as in perfect competition. Clearing the market in real life requires adequate information flows between buyer and seller to enable each buyer to match himself deliberately with the seller whose output package most closely matches his needs, and vice versa. One such information flow is the provision of advertising.

Figure 2.2 showed how these information flows can operate in the market-place. For example, buyers and sellers can physically seek each other out. When the seller is the more active of the two this was described as 'pushing' goods through the distribution channel. Alternatively buyers and sellers can employ mass communication techniques. Here, when the buyer is the more active, he advertises for tenders; when the seller is the more active, the goods are 'pulled' through the channel by customers who respond to the seller's mass advertising.*

How then can supply—demand analysis be modified to identify that quantity of advertising which will clear the market of goods? 'Quantity' of advertising has been seen to have three variants:

(a) Intensity.
(b) Extent of data variety.
(c) Style of data presentation.

At any point in time there will exist maximum and minimum limits for each of these advertising quantities.

The boundaries of advertising *intensity* can be represented by the extreme ends of two upright lines or rods, as in Fig. 6.1. *DD* is the range of possible consumer demand for advertising. At any one time the lower limit of demand for advertising is the threshold of consumer awareness of any advertising which is being directed at him. *SS*, the range of possible producer supply, must have a minimum at least equal to the lower limit of *DD* to be of any value. The upper

---

*The analysis which follows will be restricted solely to *advertising information flows* initiated by the seller. This is a simplifying assumption which ignores the many other ways in which buyers and sellers can exchange information, and which also ignores the impact on the consumer's demand for information, of varying the other elements in the marketing 'mix' such as price, distribution channel choice, other forms of promotion than advertising, and also product differentiation. This does not detract from the general validity of the ensuing discussion, but when conclusions are drawn in Chapter 8, the assumption will be relaxed, and alternative means of information transfer will also be considered.

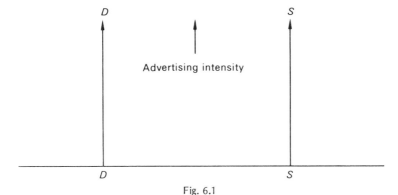

Fig. 6.1

limit to *SS* will be set by the maximum quantity of resources which firms are prepared to lay out on advertising. The upper limit to *DD* could be regarded as the level of advertising which induces ill-will rather than goodwill, as a result of overexcessive promotion.

Other things equal, profit-maximising businessmen would, of course, choose an intensity level on *SS*, corresponding to the level on *DD* where £1 more spent on advertising would result in £1 more being spent by the consumer on the advertised product. The problems this involves have already been discussed in Chapter 4. However, at this level the seller would sell all he was prepared to produce, and the market would be cleared.

The *variety* of information that consumers may want about a product, and the information that suppliers can provide, can be represented by two circles or discs of information, as in Fig. 6.2.

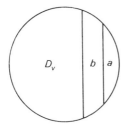 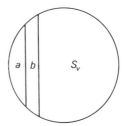

Fig. 6.2

The circumference of the left-hand disc, D_v, encloses all possible information variants that the consumer may require. The circumference of the right-hand disc, S_v, encloses all feasible varieties of data that the supplier can provide. At the limit this will amount to a fully detailed manufacturer's specification of how, and with what, the product is constructed, and under what circumstances and conditions a product will operate.

The problem is to ascertain to what extent these discs should overlap. Or, rephrasing, how much advertising should be provided so that the consumer can take a decision to purchase or to refrain from purchasing? Only when 'sufficient' data has been exchanged between the two parties will the product enter into the range of purchase options to be considered by the customer. It can then be compared with alternative purchases, subject to the normal constraints of income, preferences and so on.

Other things being equal, it is in the interests of a profit maximiser to ensure that only the optimum, not the maximum, variety of information is provided. There is nothing to be gained in spending resources on advertising to market segments where no demand, real or latent, exists for the product. For example, the maximum information required by potential car purchasers in Fig. 6.2 is D_v. For most people, however, the optimum required before deciding whether or not to buy a Rolls-Royce is probably very restricted indeed. For most, the price alone will result in a 'reject' decision. Symbolically, price information could be represented by D_v segment a. For most people, then, supply and demand for a variety of data on Rolls-Royce cars would be in equilibrium when the two discs are rotated and moved in such a way that the a segments overlap one another in identical fashion. Supply of data on miles to the gallon, acceleration levels, boot capacity and so on, contained in b segment S_v, would be a needless cost to the firm when advertising to the mass market.*

---

*Rolls-Royces *are* advertised in some mass circulation newspapers. Presumably this is because of the practical difficulties involved in totally isolating that section of the population which does want more information than merely price.

On the other hand, the optimum information required by most motorists, when seeking for points of comparison prior to choosing between an Austin or Ford, will certainly include the data provided in S_v segment *b*. In this instance, equilibrium is attained when the discs overlap precisely at *a* and *b*.

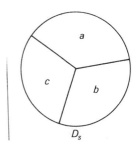 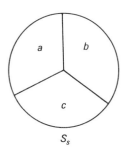

Fig. 6.3

A similar pair of information discs could contain within their boundaries all feasible *styles* of data presentation, from the least expensive to the most costly, as in Fig. 6.3. The left-hand disc D_s contains all advertising styles which might have an appeal to the relevant consumers. The right-hand disc, S_s contains all sensible methods and styles of advertising the particular product. Assume, merely for the sake of geometric simplicity, that there are only three styles, *a, b* and *c*. In practice there could be far more than three style variants, but restriction to this smaller number does not affect the nature of the argument.

The three styles could, for example, represent — in no particular order of expense — the emotional, the factual, or a combined style of approach to providing product information. The management problem is to select and supply the style which will be the most appealing to the consumer in terms of generating sales, and more importantly, profits for the advertiser. Geometrically, this involves moving and rotating the discs until the appropriate segments overlap exactly.

The threads of this discussion can now be drawn together.

Demand and supply are equated when the supply of advertising is at least equal to the minimum demand boundary in each of the three dimensions. When this occurs the following three conditions hold simultaneously:

(a) Advertising intensity levels are identical on both the *DD* and *SS* rods.
(b) The data variety discs, D_v and S_v, exactly overlap at the appropriate segments.
(c) The advertising style discs overlap at a mutually satisfactory segment.

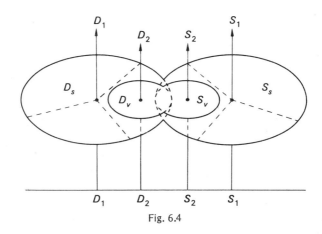

Fig. 6.4

This position is illustrated in Fig. 6.4. The four discs D_s, D_v, S_v and S_s have each been placed over an advertising intensity rod (or axle), D_1, D_2, S_2 and S_1, respectively. The discs have all settled at the same level. Thus, advertising intensity was equated.

The two discs D_v and S_v have been rotated on the appropriate rods until the relevant information variety segments exactly overlapped. Geometrically this could also have involved moving the relevant intensity rods along the horizontal plane. Thus the extent of data variety was equated.

The two larger discs D_s and S_s were similarly rotated and/or horizontally shifted until the relevant advertising styles precisely matched. In this way the style of data presentation was equated.

Unfortunately such an exact matching of supply and demand in the advertising market is not necessarily, as it would be in more conventional analysis, an optimum or equilibrium level. There is no reason why such a minimum matching will provide the appropriate volume of advertising information to clear the markets in the goods and services which are being advertised. Even if such an optimum match could be obtained it would be wrong to call it an equilibrium in the normal sense.

As with all equilibria, a businessman who perceives that he has moved away from it will try to move back towards it. If not, then he will under- or overspend on advertising to the detriment of profitability. The customer, however, will often willingly accept far more advertising information than is strictly necessary to come to a 'buy or reject' decision. This is the result of advertising being 'free' to the consumer. Customers, therefore, who are consuming more information than is adequate in this sense will not necessarily tend to demand less. Many people, for example, get a great deal of pleasure from the jingle of TV adverts or from scanning the glossy pages of luxury promotions in the weekend press supplements, but they may never intend to put such information into a purchase decision process.

The decision as to how much advertising will be 'traded' in the market is consequently only *actively* taken by suppliers. Chapter 5, however, showed how difficult it is for firms to ascertain whether they are under- or overspending on advertising. Even if no market imperfections exist on the supply side of the advertising market, even if advertisers take decisions based on profit-maximisation objectives, there will be little tendency, if advertising is set above or below some optimum, for the businessman necessarily to feel that he is in a position of disequilibrium.

The crucial problem is obviously to define the optimum level of advertising. Demand conditions for advertising may themselves be suboptimal. The minimum level of the intensity rod, *DD*, may be higher than necessary for the making of a well-informed purchase decision. More segments of the information discs D_v and D_s may require to be covered than would be expected in a Pareto optimum situation. Since suppliers' decisions are in part taken in response to demand conditions the profit-maximising advertiser must operate within any demand-imposed constraint in order to maximise returns. Such a profit maximiser might, however, increase his profits still further if the constraints imposed by demand were removed and, as a result, advertising could possibly then be reduced with no loss in sales.

4. Influences working on the Demand for Advertising

As in all other markets, supply and demand are interdependent. As a result the familiar problem arises of identifying which blade of the pair of scissors is doing the cutting at any one time. This makes it difficult, if not impossible, to conclude where equilibrium should optimally settle. In an attempt to get over this difficulty it will help to break the problem down first into component parts. The demand for advertising will vary, for example, with the following characteristics of either the product or the consumer:

(a) The simplicity or complexity of the product advertised.
(b) The rate of change of technology, style or the conditions of sale.
(c) The level of skill, or conversely, inexperience of the purchaser.
(d) The degree of stability or mobility of the population of potential buyers.
(e) The extent of variation of product types.
(f) The proportion of total expenditure by the purchaser on the relevant article.

(a) Product Complexity

Other things equal, the more complex is the product to use or maintain, then the greater is the variety of information required. Contrast, for example, the information required by potential buyers of two similar kitchen appliances, a refrigerator and a washing machine. Price and storage capacity are important to refrigerator buyers. Otherwise, operation of the machine merely requires connection to the nearest electrical socket. A washing machine buyer, however, will want to know not only price and load capacity, but will need assurance that the controls are easy to understand, that service engineers are readily available, that the machine is easy to 'plumb in', and so on.

Casual observation of advertisements for these two product types supports this argument. Firms feel compelled to react to consumer demand by overlapping the D_v and S_v circles to a much greater extent in the case of washing machines.

The argument is not only intuitively attractive but can be supported by the use of conventional economic theory. In neoclassical theory the consumer will always buy such an amount of a product that its marginal utility is equal to its price. (2) Marginal utility, however, is essentially a subjective measure in this context. In lay terms the equation merely states that, while a consumer may have a conscious need for a washing machine, he will only buy it if it is 'worth the money'. This subjective worth or marginal utility of a washing machine will depend on the consumer's assessment of the product. To assess a washing machine requires more information than to assess a refrigerator.

In other words, if more complex products are more heavily advertised than simpler items, *ceteris paribus*, this is a refelection of consumer demand for advertising as he attempts to optimise his expenditure decisions, rather than the result of some factor on the supply side of the market.

(b) Changes in the Conditions of Sale
Some markets are more dynamic than others. New products may be introduced more often, or prices changed more frequently. Any assessment a consumer may have made to ascertain if price equals marginal utility will be outdated as a result of each change. Prior to making a purchase decision the consumer will have to make a fresh and appropriate assessment. More information will be required for this assessment, and high levels of advertising in such markets may again merely reflect the activities of consumers striving to allocate their spending in the most subjectively satisfying pattern.

This probably explains the high frequency of grocery store advertising in the local press towards weekends. Food prices change frequently, and the housewife wants to know where the most satisfactory suppliers of her weekend meat, butter and egg purchases are located. In a similar manner, consumers in markets with a high rate of style change or a high level of new product introductions will find their evaluations of purchase possibilities rapidly rendered redundant. This redundancy can only be avoided if they search for further information about the changed conditions of sale in the market (i.e. demand more advertising). This argument possibly partly* explains the trend of promotion in the soap powder market. In 1954, the year of the introduction of the new synthetic detergents, Unilever's selling expenses were equal to 36 per cent of sales turnover. This was double the 1952 figure and well above the 'normal level of around a quarter of sales value thereafter'. (3)

(c) The Experience of the Purchaser
Increased dexterity by dint of repetition is not confined to Adam Smith's well-known pin makers. The more frequently a purchase decision is made, the more knowledgeable the consumer becomes about conditions in the market-place, the closer to optimal will his decisions become. For this reason it is often argued that the industrial buyer who is a professional purchaser will require far less advertising than the consumer buyer. This is not a strictly fair comparison.

The professional purchaser will certainly require little additional information about day to day purchasing of basic materials in markets with fairly stable conditions of sale. But neither will the housewife buying chocolate bars for her children. The professional purchaser, however, would require considerably more product information if he were buying,

---

*Innovation also affects the *supply* of advertising. No attempt is made here to identify which of the two, supply or demand, it most affects. The discussion is developed further in Chapter 7. Whether or not particular style changes merit consumer search for information about them has been discussed in Chapter 3.

say, a replacement machine for the first time in a twelve-month period. Similarly, so would the housewife buying a child's new suit of clothes.

Skill in purchasing, therefore, depends on experience rather than on training. Repetitive purchases provide the buyer with knowledge which Stigler has called 'accumulated search'. (4) The greater the quantity of accumulated search, the less advertising will be demanded.

This conclusion on 'advertising quantity' however, is only applicable to the 'intensity' and 'data variety' dimensions, not to the 'data style'. There is no reason to suppose, for example, that the businessman who gets pleasure from expensively styled adverts in the weekend colour supplements will not prefer similarly styled advertisements for, say, component parts in his appropriate trade journal. Where the D_s disc will settle is not a function of buyer experience, but of personality and mood of the buyer. So, for this particular dimension of advertising quantity, we cannot make any *a priori* predictions of whether it will be high or low as a consequence of purchaser skill.

(d) Buyer Population Stability
New entrants to a market will have no previous experience or accumulated search to draw on. They will consequently have a high demand level for the information which advertising can provide. All markets have such new entrants. In prescription medicines there is the fresh graduate output of doctors each year from the universities. In household furniture there is the continuous flow of newly-weds. In other consumer durables, such as cars or hi-fi equipment, there are the large sections of the population with rising incomes and aspiration levels which take in such products as purchase possibilities for the first time.

All such new entrants will have colleagues, friends and instructors from whom they can gain advice and vicarious experience. Nonetheless such advice and experience is equally available to existing market members, as well as to new entrants. Under similar circumstances therefore, the more new entrants a market has, either because of market growth

or membership turnover, the more advertising that market
will demand.

In this case 'more' advertising will certainly refer to data
variety. New entrants will demand a wider variety of data
than will experienced buyers. But 'more' will not necessarily
refer to style of advertising. There is no reason why a more or
a less expensive style of advertising should be demanded in
such markets. Clearly the style of advertising must have the
appropriate appeal to meet the demand of new entrants. New
consumers will be strange to the market-place and will
consequently be searching for a style of reassurance to
remove the psychological discomfort of unfamiliarity.
Whether or not meeting this demand is costly or inexpensive,
however, can only be judged on the merits of the case.
Advertising intensity, however, may well be increased with a
high level of buyer mobility. The demand of new market
entrants for various products will, in many instances, still be
latent rather than actual. For example, a 16-year-old, taking
home his first wage packet may have little understanding of
the advantages of opening his own bank account. Such a 'new
entrant' may pay little attention to bank advertising, feeling
that it has little relevance for him. As a result, the new
entrant's threshold of awareness to advertising may well be
higher than in the case of established and frequent product
purchasers. To get over this threshold, the foot of the
intensity rod *SS* must be raised to the relatively high
minimum level of the *DD* rod.

(e) Product Differentiation
The wider the range of similar product types facing the
consumer, the greater will be the data variety demanded.
When only one product faces the consumer, information
need only be sufficient to enable a purchase or reject decision
to be taken. When a range of products faces the consumer,
and a purchase decision has been made, the problem of
choice between alternatives still remains. Additional information will be demanded by the consumer as he attempts to
optimise that choice.

This is not, of course, a reason why greater intensity or a
costlier style of advertising should be demanded. But

certainly, in at least the dimension of data variety, *advertising can be expected to be higher in conditions of product differentiation because of consumer need.* *

(f) The Price—Income Ratio

The price—income ratio indicates the proportion of consumer income which a particular purchase would absorb. Convenience goods such as foodstuffs, newspapers and cigarettes will generally have a low ratio. Consumer durables and more expensive luxuries will have a high ratio. In industrial purchasing a similar comparison could be made between, say, loose tools and an important raw material.

It can be postulated that the higher is the ratio then the greater is the consumer awareness of the value of advertising to aid choice. When the ratio is low the opportunity cost in terms of a faulty decision resulting in income foregone is small. It will not appear to be worthwhile to demand a high level of advertising or to go to the effort of seeking out and sifting a high level of information to avoid a possibly suboptimal decision. When the ratio is high, however, the penalties of making a wrong decision cannot be so readily ignored. It may only cost a consumer 1p more for a box of chocolates if he fails to search for the cheapest sweet shop in the locality, but failure to locate the cheapest licensed grocer may result in him paying 35p more for a bottle of whisky.

It can be argued, then, that high consumer awareness of the value of advertising when the price—income ratio is high implies that the threshold level of intensity required for advertising to be noted is low. Other things equal, the foot of the *DD* rod will be at a relatively low level when the price—income ratio is high. If this is so, then this argument is in agreement with those studies which have shown that low-priced consumer goods tend to have a higher advertising—sales ratio than higher-priced goods. (5)

Conversely the quantity of advertising demanded, as

---

*This explanation differs radically from the more frequently made charge that advertising is high in conditions of product differentiation because *suppliers* wish to exploit or enhance such differences in order to render demand less elastic and so permit the charging of higher prices.

measured by data variety, will be higher when the price—
income ratio is high. Consumers will actively want to
undertake relatively more extensive product comparisons
when the cost of a wrong decision would be high. This is at
least one reason why such products may have a higher
absolute advertising cost *per purchase* than lower price—
income ratio goods.

The costliness of the advertising style to be used, again
depends more on the personalities of buyers in the product
markets than on the price—income ratio. There is no reason
to assume that these are related.

The discussion of this whole section can now be summarised. Table 6.1 shows how the quantity demanded of
advertising was argued to vary with each of the six
parameters.

Table 6.1. *Direction of demand variation*

Market characteristic	Quantity dimension	Advertising intensity	Data variety	Advertising style
Complex products		Indeterminate	Directly	Indeterminate
Variable conditions of sale		Directly	Directly	Indeterminate
Inexperienced purchasers		Directly	Directly	Indeterminate
Mobile buyer population		Directly	Directly	Indeterminate
Product differentiation		Indeterminate	Directly	Indeterminate
High price—income ratio		Inversely	Directly	Indeterminate

5. What is Excess Demand?

Eighteen ways in which the demand for advertising can vary
were examined (six market characteristics, three dimensions
of demand). In ten cases out of eighteen, reasons have been
put forward for understanding why and how demand will
vary. Table 6.1, however, still displays two glaring omissions.

Firstly, no guide is given as to when an inexpensive style
and when a costly style of advertising is liable to be
demanded.

Secondly, no guide is given as to what the optimum upper
level of demand will be in any of its three dimensions.
Demand will be higher in some conditions and lower in

others. No guide is given as to *how much* higher it will be in such conditions.

Consumers will not demand more than they want, but since advertising is 'free' they may well demand more than they would need for optimal purchase decision taking. This, in turn, may result in resources being diverted towards advertising and, correspondingly, away from other industries, at a net social loss.

Unfortunately the observer can only define the upper limits to demand for intensity and variety. After a point, over-intense advertising can result in negative returns to the advertiser. People are ceasing to demand advertising at that point. Similarly, over-effusive data variety in advertisements may result in consumer confusion or, possibly, refusal to assimilate the information. Again, negative returns to the advertising set in at this point; people are ceasing to demand. Prior to these levels, however, consumers may cheerfully accept more intense advertising and more detailed advertising than is necessary for decision taking. Interest in the advertisements themselves — for amusement, general knowledge or whatever motivation — may keep demand above the optimal.

The optimum level of expenditure on advertising style to meet demand is even more difficult to define. Again, the advertiser must not choose an inappropriate style given knowledge of the intended target of the advertisements. The 'appropriateness' of style, however, is not necessarily a function of the level of expenditure. (For example, both the factual and emotional approaches to advertising could be undertaken either frugally or lavishly in expenditure terms.) However, once the appropriate style has been selected, the expenditure to be laid out on it to satisfy demand is almost impossible to define.

Given that style is meant to appeal to the potential market, the scope to lay out money on attractive, entertaining advertisements with a particular style of approach is vast. With fixed advertising intensity and data variety, there is no rational reason why spending more money on style, namely, consumer appeal or entertainment, should ever reach a point of consumer satisfaction. The limits would be set only by the level of intensity chosen. (For example, one cannot spend more than some finite amount, however large, on creating an attractive colour film with a well-paid cast of actors, for a 60-second TV advertisement.)

The observer is left with the suspicion that more advertising *will be* demanded that is optimal, due to its being in joint supply with the products it promotes, and so effectively, being sold at a zero price. The responsibility for levels of advertising must not then be laid at the doors of consumers, but rather, at those of the *active* decision makers in the market for advertising, the suppliers. The ways in which suppliers select levels of advertising have been examined. Factors in the market for advertising which affect these internal decisions will be looked at in the next chapter.

7 Conditions affecting the Supply of Advertising

Advertising levels depend on more than the nature of demand for information. Supply conditions are also important. This chapter examines four variables influencing the supply of advertising: first, economies of scale in production; second, innovation; third, market power and psychological considerations. Finally, we shall consider what is meant by oversupply of advertising.

1. Economies of Scale

Average total cost (ATC) can only be reduced by advertising where average advertising cost (AAC) is less than the savings per unit obtained in average production cost (APC) when the scale of production is increased. If APC is constant or rising, then any advertising must raise ATC, since advertising itself adds to the costs. The two alternative situations are illustrated in Figs. 7.1a and b. In both diagrams Q_1 represents output before advertising, Q_2 output after advertising. Even Fig. 7.1a does not give an unambiguous answer, of course. Had output only been raised to Q_3, then ATC would have risen from AC_1 to AC_3.

Nothing can be deduced about the influence of advertising

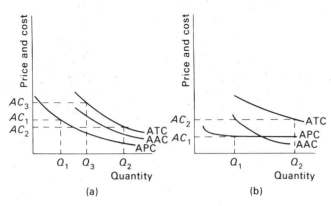

Fig. 7.1

on total unit costs *a priori*, but the possibility of achieving scale economies deserves investigation. For example, it has been claimed that heavy advertising of synthetic household detergents made possible lower costs per unit of output than would otherwise have been obtained. The huge blowing towers used in the manufacture of detergent powders only attain minimum unit cost at an output of 70,000 tons a year, equal to approximately one-fifth of the total U.K. market. At this level of output, unit production costs are one-half those of a plant producing 28,000 tons per year. Given such economies in manufacture and given similar but less spectacular ones in packaging and bulk buying, it has been estimated that a smaller producer of detergent powders *who undertook no advertising or product research* would still have average total costs above those of a large supplier who did incur such expenditures. (1) This does not imply that advertising of detergents does not exceed the level needed to attain these economies of scale.

A further *caveat* must also be presented. Advertising may increase a firm's demand and lower its ATC, but if this increase has been obtained at the expense of competitors rather than from an increase in total industry demand, then any movement towards lower costs in one firm will tend to be cancelled out within the industry due to a reverse movement in other firm's costs. Unless these other firms are driven out of business, and demand concentrated only on those firms able to reap the relevant scale economies, then the average of unit costs throughout the industry may not fall, as postulated. Whether cost differences due to advertising will or will not lead to corresponding price differences cannot be determined merely by examining the direction in which costs have moved. If advertising has resulted in lower costs the new equilibrium price will depend upon what has happened to marginal receipts, as well as what has happened to marginal costs. The outcome may, but need not necessarily, be a lower price. (The determination of optimal price, output, quality and advertising levels was discussed in Chapter 4).

2. Innovation
It was noted in Chapter 6 that the demand for knowledge of a product varies with the mobility of members of the pool of potential purchasers. The more new arrivals into the pool, the more information and the more advertising is required. Similar reasoning can be applied to illustrate why innovations receive heavier promotional backing than established products. When a new product is launched the entire market must be informed. Existing patterns of goodwill must be broken down. Consumer ignorance, suspicion, inertia and insecurity about trying 'something different' must be overcome. More advertising is required to induce people to try something new than to repeat a purchase. Rivals try to prevent changes in consumption patterns by increased promotion or price reductions until they too can introduce a satisfactory substitute. High levels of advertising are therefore to be expected as the innovator struggles to attain a high initial level of goodwill.

The pattern of advertising for pharmaceuticals illustrates the relationship of advertising to innovation. Figure 7.2 shows the weight of advertising concentrated on the introduction of new products. After launch, promotion expenditure falls off to a low reminder level. Sales are maintained, however, by the continued effects of the initial promotion.

This evidence supports those writers who have pointed out that current sales do not depend on current advertising

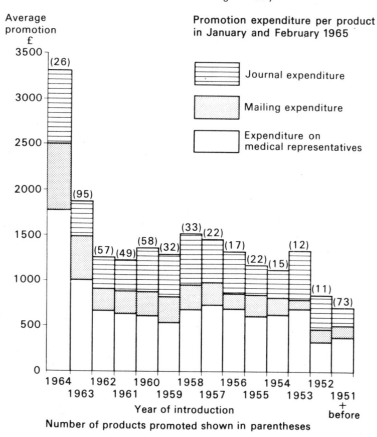

Promotional Expenditure Per Product Promoted by Age of Product in the U.K. Drug Industry

Average promotion £

Promotion expenditure per product in January and February 1965

Journal expenditure

Mailing expenditure

Expenditure on medical representatives

Year of introduction

Number of products promoted shown in parentheses

Fig. 7.2

Source: G. Teeling-Smith, *Innovation and the Balance of Payments: the Experience in the Pharmaceutical Industry* Office of Health Economics, 1968, p. 65.

expenditure. Rather, they depend on the accumulated effects of past expenditures. (2) Were no reminder advertising to take place one would expect the initial promotion to continue to provide future sales but with diminishing effectiveness as purchasers gradually forgot and competitors attracted their attention. Waugh (3) has used the concept of a 'decay curve' to illustrate this effect of current advertising on future sales, an effect which shows a decline or 'decay' in future sales year by year unless reminder advertising is undertaken. He postulated that the current effects of advertising 'typically are small in relation to the total effect'. Hoos (4) put forward a similar view suggesting that 'promotion inputs may have an effct on demand in subsequent periods in addition to or in place of the period when the promotion is injected'.

Reminder advertising, however, as may be seen from Fig. 7.2, can be at a much lower level than the initial expenditure. Once the 'capital expenditure' has been made and goodwill attained, all that is required in future periods is relatively low 'capital maintenance' outlay.

Again, riders must be added to the argument that advertising will be higher where there is innovation. Firstly, the establishment of this case in general is much easier than selecting a specific level of promotional activity which is deemed optimal. Second, the fact that advertising enables new products to gain a foothold in the market may in turn encourage firms to proliferate 'needless' product modifications, which in turn will be heavily promoted in order to gain a competitive march on their rivals.

3. Market Power

Advertising changes the position and shape of a firm's demand curve. In other words, it increases a firm's market power by further separating its market from those of its competitors. The extent of the market power may be measured by (a) the height to which price may be raised without inducing new suppliers to enter the market, (b) the degree of seller concentration, (c) the stability of market shares.

(a) Price Levels

Anyone who has compared the price of Aspirin B.P. with that of a heavily advertised brand, such as 'Aspro', will be prepared to believe that advertised goods sell at higher prices. The most careful comparison of prices for non-advertised and advertised products was made by Telser. (5) He confirmed

that, within product classes, advertised goods generally sell at
higher prices than non-advertised 'equivalents'. He argued,
however, that such prices differences need not imply abuse of
market power as the differences often did no more than
reflect higher or more reliable quality.
Certainly if consumers do not get some tangible or
intangible satisfaction from a higher-priced brand there is no
reason why such products should continue to exist side by
side with less-well advertised ones. Whether or not we as
individuals approve of the intangible satisfactions that other
individuals obtain in this way is another matter. This is a
different problem whose ticklish nature can best be illustrated by posing a series of questions. Firstly, are consumers
unable to judge what are their own best interests when
confronted with a high-priced, high-advertised brand and a
low-priced, non-advertised substitute? Second, if not, who is
to judge what these 'best interests' are? The answer to this
second question can be at least threefold: successfully
persuasive advertisers; successfully persuasive price cutters;
successfully persuasive self-appointed arbiters of choice.
Third, are any of these bodies likely to act in the long run as
reliably for the consumers' interests as the consumer himself?
   Some argue that self-interest is a less dangerous force than
self-righteousness. Others disagree. Unfortunately all views in
this area still rest to a greater or lesser extent on prejudice,
and one man's prejudice is no better than another's.

(b) Seller Concentration
High concentration could lead to heavy advertising, or heavy
advertising could lead to high market concentration. *A priori*
there is no reason for the causality to run in one direction
rather than the other. The relationship, therefore, deserves
closer consideration. Reasons why concentrated industries
undertake a lot of advertising are examined first of all. First,
oligopoly theory indicates that price competition is unlikely
where competitors are few. Under such circumstances
businessmen will place relatively more stress on promotion
and/or product differentiation as tactics of interfirm rivalry.
Taplin emphasises this relationship between oligopoly and
advertising. He writes that 'it is a consequence of the

limitation of competition . . . heavy advertising expenditures are incurred by a few large producers . . . kept at it by the fear that the first one to stop will simply be leaving his competitors to go ahead and steal his market.' (6)

Secondly, concentrated markets are often made up of large firms with financial resources sufficient for the high absolute expense of advertising. Thirdly, products are often differentiated and need to have their special features drawn to the attention of buyers. Despite Emerson's assertion that the world will make a beaten path to the better mousetrap manufacturer, the world will first have to be told of its (differentiated) existence. Finally, since all advertising benefits both the firm which advertises and the broad commodity group within which the advertised product lies, the larger the firm the greater proportionately is the return it gets of the *total* commodity group benefits provided by its own promotion. Firms with large market shares are therefore likely to get a greater return per pound spent on promotion.

On the other hand, it may be argued that high levels of concentration lead to high levels of advertising. Kaldor writes that advertising, by switching demand from one firm to another, tends to benefit larger firms with greater 'pulling power' at the expense of smaller, and thus encourages a tendency towards oligopolistic concentration. (7) If, as we have argued, larger firms have a relative advantage over smaller in advertising because they capture more of the effect of the advertising for their own products, then advertising will lead to the growth of the larger firms, i.e. to greater concentration. Small firms may be further handicapped by lack of finance for advertising and decline in size.

Finally, a similar but less rapid process may occur if there are substantial scale economies in advertising. For example, low-circulation journals or newspapers frequently have lower absolute insertion costs than high-circulation periodicals. However, it is cost per contact that matters to an advertiser, and when the relevant insertion cost is divided by circulation (or readership) the cost per contact may be substantially higher in the low-circulation publication; but smaller firms may only be able to afford low absolute insertion costs. In a similar vein, larger firms may not only achieve lower cost per contact, but also lower cost per *effective* contact, as they are able to indulge in repetitive advertising till a threshold level of consumer attention is attained and they may be able to employ people with greater skill and creativeness to design their adverts.

Telser, in the article already cited, made one of the first attempts to ascertain what relationship exists between advertising and market concentration. He compared advertising intensity (i.e. advertising—sales ratios) with market concentration data for forty-two industries. The correlation he discovered between the two was 'unimpressive'. A more recent study based on a differently constructed sample of fourteen industries, however, found a significant and strong statistical association between advertising intensity and concentration. (8) This resulted in a controversy, with both sets of authors defending their respective conclusions and the statistical bases on which they rested. (9)

At least two points were left largely unconsidered by both sets of protagonists. One was the nature of the relationship between the two variables and entry barriers (discussed in the next section). The second was the fact that interindustry differences in advertising depend on several other factors, in addition to market concentration. On the supply side of an industry these factors include the level of innovation and the extent to which products are manufactured with a view to producing relatively tangible or intangible consumer satisfactions. On the demand side of the industry the level of advertising will vary according to the demand for knowledge of the product, which in turn is dependent on the wide variety of variables already examined in Chapter 6.

This writer attempted to meet these criticisms in a study of thirty-seven markets within the British pharmaceutical industry. (10) The study used a cross-sectional multiple regression analysis carried out on pharmaceutical advertising at the level of the therapeutic submarket. In economic terms the therapeutic submarkets are the segments of the total pharmaceutical market between which the cross-elasticity of demand for competing products is very low. (For example, antidiarrhoeals cannot be used as cardiovascular agents, nor antibiotics as contraceptives.) It is in these areas, not the

total market, that study of market power is most meaningful.
It is probable that conditions on both the supply and
demand side of each of these markets were very similar to
those in every other market. The firms participating in each
were all members of the pharmaceutical industry. Production
techniques in each market were not dissimilar, and scale
economies were largely absent (11) (except that fermentation
is required in the case of antibiotics, but even here, firms can
buy in the finished chemical and encapsulate it or present it
in some other suitable proprietary form). The customers
operating in each market were all members of the medical
profession, and since the sales data used were restricted to
general practitioners and did not include hospital specialists,
these customers would all participate to a more or less similar
extent in each market. Some other dissimilarities between the
submarkets were, of course, inevitable (e.g. the level of
innovation and the state of technology in each). An attempt
was made to take these variables into consideration also in
the analysis, and this is reported more fully later in Section 4.

The results obtained suggested that there is no relationship
between market structure and advertising. However, although
some of the difficulties involved in making valid interindustry
comparisons were overcome, the exercise related overall to
only one industry, pharmaceuticals, and it would be dangerous
to generalise from one industry. It seems likely that the general
picture will have to be built up by such industry case studies,
rather than by cross-sectional econometric analysis, which so
often is unable to embrace all the relevant variables.

(c) Barriers to Entry
A more fundamental criticism of the above approach is that
it is fallacious to relate advertising with market structure in
an attempt to establish the relationship between advertising
and market power.

It is often argued that higher concentration, *ceteris
paribus*, will lead to higher profit levels than will a lower level
of concentration. However, other things are not always equal,
and if entry barriers are low then it will be less likely that an
industry's price levels will long exceed average cost. One way
of raising prices, and so profits, is to raise entry barriers with

104   *Advertising*

the assistance of advertising. (This argument was given strong support by Joe S. Bain in his *Barriers to New Competition*). If one wants to ascertain what relation exists between market power and advertising one should examine advertising's relationship with profit rates, not with concentration levels. Although concentration may lead to higher profits when barriers to entry are sufficiently high, these barriers need not be raised by advertising: other entry barriers are adequate. In other words, concentration and advertising are variables which are independent one of the other. It would not, consequently, be surprising to find little statistical relationship between them even if market power and advertising *are* strongly associated. High profit rates, the fruits of market power, may be dependent on both these (independent) variables.

Figure 7.3 provides a summary of the considerations leading businessmen to advertise in order to permit the level of the entry-deterring price to be raised. *L* is the entry-deterring or limit price in the absence of advertising, where entry barriers are limited to scale economies or absolute cost

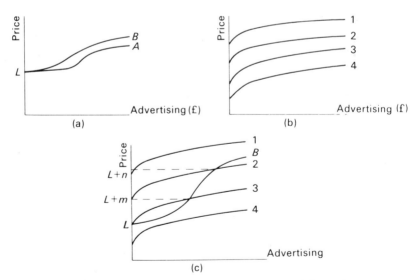

Fig. 7.3. *(a) How the limit price may vary with advertising (b) Sales isoquants at different price–advertising combinations (c) Maintenance of output and raising of price through advertising.*

advantages. In the absence of advertising, entry will occur if price is raised above L. If only a small amount of advertising is engaged in, the limit price will be little affected since the advertising will not be particularly effective, or if it is, entrants will find it easy to equal. This is illustrated in Fig. 7.3a by the relatively flat shape of the curve LB (plotting entry-deterring price) when only a small movement has been made along the x- or advertising axis. As existing firms increase their advertising, however, new entrants would also have to incur substantial advertising investment in order to break down existing firms' goodwill, while simultaneously creating their own. This makes it possible for existing firms to charge a higher price than L without attracting entry, and the entry-deterring price curve LB rises quite sharply. After a point, diminishing returns to advertising may set in, and the curve begins to level off. Curve LA has a similar, but gentler shape. This curve would apply in industries where advertising is not so effective as an entry barrier (e.g. compare cigarettes, where brand loyalty induced by advertising is high, with flour sales to the bakery trade, where customer choice is made largely on the basis of price or service).

Figure 7.3b is a group of equal output curves. Each is a locus of price-selling expense combinations which are capable of inducing sales of the same output level. They slope upwards from left to right initially, because more advertising is required to sell the same output at higher prices. After a point, increasing advertising is less effective as a compensating mechanism for price increases, and the slope becomes less steep. Figure 7.3c superimposes the previous two diagrams, one on the other. This shows how a firm originally producing quantity 3 at price L can raise its price to level $L + m$ without inducing entry, while maintaining constant output. (Price could be raised still further to $L + n$, but in this instance, sales would have to be forfeited by moving from isoquant 3 to isoquant 2.)

Comanor and Wilson, (12) inspired by arguments similar to these, carried out a multivariate analysis on a sample of forty-one consumer goods industries. They discovered that industries with a high advertising outlay, and so high entry barriers, earned profit rates nearly half as high again as the other industries in their sample. It should be pointed out,

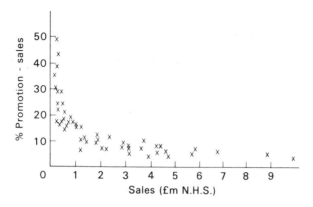

Fig. 7.4. *Promotion—sales ratios compared with firm size*
Source: W. Duncan Reekie, *The Economics of Innovation with Special Reference to the British Pharmaceutical Industry* (A.B.P.I., 1971) p. 30.

however, that Camanor and Wilson used data from companies' published accounts to carry out their study. But profits computed by accountants do not reflect the creation of long term market goodwill by advertising. Such goodwill is an asset to a company. To the extent that this asset is not recorded in a firm's balance sheet then the assets of firms with high advertising are understated and, as a consequence, profit rates as a return on capital employed are exaggerated.

Figure 7.4 illustrates how sales expenditures discourage firms from entering the pharmaceutical industry on a nationwide scale. It will be seen that, at low levels of sales, promotion expenditures are very high relative to sales. Promotion is regarded by firms in the industry as an activity which must be conducted at some minimum absolute level, irrespective of size of company. The threshold level of advertising, below which little or no results are obtained, lay close to £100,000 per annum in 1966. The effect of this threshold level on the smaller firm is clearly visible. In attempting to obtain viable levels of promotion, the smaller firms were forced to expend sums ranging up to almost 50 per cent of sales income. This cannot but deter small firms from entering the industry and must make the continued operation of existing small firms precarious.

The ability to raise price above the limit level is not

necessarily bad from a social point of view. It may enable scale economies to be reaped by preventing fragmentation of the market among too many firms; it may provide the finance for carrying out research and development, and so on. Again it is difficult to judge. Posing a series of questions may again help clarify thought. Do consumers have freedom to choose from a variety of firms? Does this freedom include the ability to choose lower-priced items? If there is not such a choice, then a small number of firms can dominate the market and charge excessively high prices, and there may be no obligation on them to pass on the benefits of improved technology or scale economies.

If advertising raises the entry deterring price so that entry is unlikely, and oligopolists compete by promotion not by price, then what Taplin called a 'particularly vicious circle' is set up. Price cannot fall far if advertising costs are to be met, and the consumer must pay for the advertising or do without the product.

Both the consumer and the advertiser may dislike this state of affairs, but there will be little either can do. The oligopolist will be frightened to cut his advertising for fear that his competitors can then go ahead and capture his market. Oligopoly, then, may not only be 'price sticky', as the theory of the kinked demand curve suggests, but may also be 'advertising sticky', and that at a high level.

How can we tell if this lack of choice exists and so compels purchase of high-priced, heavily advertised brands? Few answers are satisfactory. One approach is to ascertain if, at least, opportunities for choice do vary over time. Does entry in fact occur? Are firms' market shares affected by shifting consumers' preferences? Or can advertising ensure stable market shares over time?

(d) Market Share Stability
Telser (5) used market share data based on consumer recall interviews to ascertain whether advertising could stabilise a firm's market share. He compared share stability for three groups of products: a heavily advertised group (toiletries), a less heavily advertised group (soaps), and a group with low advertising intensity (foods). Over the three points in time chosen, 1948, 1953 and 1959, the most stable shares were

held by food products, followed by soaps. He alleges 'these
results refute the view that advertising stabilises market
shares'. The results are explained on the grounds that there is
more frequent innovation in toiletries than in foods, and that
the higher advertising levels are symptomatic of rivalry
between products, rather than a drive for share stability.
They certainly give no support to the thesis that advertising
diminishes competition. It would be interesting, however, to
carry out similar exercises *within, rather than between,
product groups* in order to eliminate the effects of interindustry differences in advertising levels. It would also be
interesting to carry out similar exercises for firms rather than
for brands. Otherwise, is it not possible to look on a market
rather as a game of unlosable musical chairs? When the music
stops, the brands participating in the game have changed, but
the number of chairs have remained unaltered, and each firm
merely substitutes new brands for its displaced products.

4. Products providing Intangible Satisfaction

Where the intrinsic product is perfectly homogeneous,
theory — as Dorfman and Steiner (13) pointed out — gives no
guidance as to whether advertising will be zero or positive. It
will be positive if firms attempt to associate intangible
satisfactions with the product, zero if they do not. But most
products, even those which sell largely on the strengths of
intangible values, do have some real and important differences,
albeit possibly ones which are difficult to measure. (Although
the president of Revlon Cosmetics was the first to admit that
'they sold hope', few would disagree that Revlon's products
also differ from other cosmetics in colour, smell and
consistency, however slightly.) When this is so, then theory
tends to indicate that the supply of advertising will be relatively
high.*

---

*The Dorfman-Steiner theorem states that profit maximising equilibrium will
occur when the price elasticity of demand, η, equals the marginal value product of
advertising, μ. Where the product differences are important, but difficult to assess,
then η has a low value. Simultaneously, consumer uncertainty about products will
raise the value of μ. Until advertising has reached a sufficiently high absolute value
for diminishing returns to set in, and so for μ to fall towards η, equilibrium will fail
to be attained. This is exemplified in Dorfman and Steiner's diagram 1(B), where

This author attempted to test this theory in the pharmaceutical industry. Some writers have suggested that firms in that industry use misleading claims in order to strengthen the persuasive element of advertising. (14) If this is so, then it might be argued that advertising would be heaviest in those areas where misleading claims are less readily detectable. This argument can be extended to promotion by advertisers who would otherwise shun intentional dishonesty. For example, there are still many disease areas where the therapy available is symptom relieving, not curative, and possibly fails to meet even this former claim. In such areas more persuasion is possibly required to get doctors to prescribe than in markets where drugs have well-defined and easily recognisable medical effects. As Ansoff put it, there may be 'an appropriate Parkinson's Law to the effect that advertising budget spent on a product is in inverse ratio to the precision with which its mission can be specified.' (15) With fewer specific claims to promote, firms are left with the alternative of shouting louder. Furthermore there may tend to be a very low level of brand loyalty in such areas, as doctors search for the most effective remedy or, knowing that this is an unlikely attainment, switch patients from one product to another in the hope of obtaining at least the most successful placebo. 'It is a reasonable conjecture that products with a low level of loyalty and hard core, call for higher advertising budgets than in the case of products with higher loyalties.' (16)

These arguments could suggest that in disease areas where background knowledge is low and medicines have imprecise

---

the relevant curves have the following shape:

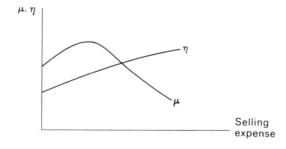

effects, then promotion will be relatively high, as producers attempt to sell drugs with relatively little to commend them other than the weight of promotion itself.

It was postulated that the level of advertising, A_t, in each submarket would be associated with the following variables:

(a) the degree of market concentration, M.
(b) the level of sales that firms anticipated from their advertising efforts, $\bar{S}_t$;
(c) the level of innovation, I;
(d) the ability to use misleading claims — or the inability to make precise ones, D.

As mentioned earlier, no association was discovered with market concentration. However, statistically significant associations were discovered with each of the other three variables, including variable D. (This variable was inserted into the equation as a dummy representing the state of technology in each submarket. Expert pharmacological and medical advice was sought on the matter, and values of zero were attributed to areas with a 'very well developed' state of technology and 'one' to areas where it was 'less developed'.)

Thus this evidence supports the theory that the supply of advertising will be greater where products provide intangible, rather than concrete benefits.

5. What is Oversupply?

This chapter and Chapter 6 have discussed many of the determinants of the levels of advertising in industry. Businessmen take decisions on the activity according to their assessment of the demand for advertising by consumers, and to the conditions in their respective industries surrounding its supply. Given the assumption that businessmen are profit maximisers,* they will spend on advertising until they estimate that the marginal revenue to be gained from the activity equals its marginal cost. Given the demand and supply conditions for the industry, this may well lead to some sort of optimum level of expenditure.

---

*This is not necessarily so, but the implications for decision making were discussed in Chapter 4.

However, there are at least three main reasons why even this 'sort of optimum' may not be attained, and advertising be instead at a still higher level. First, the techniques available to businessmen to gauge the effectiveness of their advertising and in turn to assess the worth of any particular level or levels of expenditure are still in the early stages of development. In consequence, decisions must be taken on the basis of inadequate knowledge, and expenditure will, more often than not, either exceed or fail to reach the optimal level. (Chapters 4 and 5 were devoted to examining the currently available range of decision-making tools that advertising managers have access to, and to suggesting how, in many cases, economic analysis can aid rational decision making.)

Second, as already argued, in oligopoly situations, prices may not only be 'sticky' (as suggested by the price theorists' kinked demand curve), but advertising expenditure may also be stable. There were noted to be good reasons for thinking that this 'stability' would end up at a higher rather than a lower level than optimal, from both consumers' and producers' viewpoints. Whether or not the vicious ratchet effect this argument implies can be curbed, either by cartel-like self-discipline in the industry itself or by Monopolies Commission policing or other government policy, will be examined in Chapter 8.

Third, because advertising is a free good, or at least has its 'price' to the consumer, embedded and effectively concealed in the product it is related to, it can be argued that more of it will be demanded, and so supplied, than would be the case if it were supplied as a separate commodity with an identifiable price. The implication of this argument for policy will also be looked at in Chapter 8.

The question remains, if oversupply does exist, can it be readily identified? There are very few practical tools available to help decide at what point an industry's advertising level becomes wasteful: Interindustry and interfirm comparisons are two frequently used methods. However, these can only claim validity if the supply and demand conditions for each of the compared entities are rendered constant in some way. Furthermore, conditions within the firms or industries compared must also be similar. Two similar industries may spend similar amounts on advertising, yet the place which advertising occupies in their respective total marketing mixes may be important in the one, yet insignificant in the other, e.g. in the ice-cream and detergent industries referred to in Chapter 3. At times, however, intermarket or interfirm comparisons may be very useful in highlighting advertising levels which are higher than might otherwise be expected.

For example, in the study of the thirty-seven therapeutic submarkets in the pharmaceutical industry, the following statistically significant estimating equation was obtained:

$$A_t = 18.938I + 0.029\bar{S}_t + 56.666D + 4.146$$

When the promotion figure for antibiotics was estimated from this equation, it was found that the actual 1966 promotion figure exceeded its estimated value by 30 per cent. It was concluded that this unusually high discrepancy was primarily due to the large size of the antibiotics submarket, relative to the other 36. (Antibiotics is by far the largest submarket, accounting for almost one-fifth of total industry sales.) The rivalry between firms in antibiotics is such that, lured on by the relatively vast prizes of shares in the turnover of this market, they spend a disproportionately large amount on antibiotics advertising. Antibiotics promotion is unexpectedly, and perhaps unnecessarily, high.

The antibiotics example provides yet another example of the pitfalls which can lie in wait for the unwary who attempt to condemn or condone 'excessive' advertising levels. What is the appropriate measure of 'excess'? Expenditure on advertising per pound of sales, or outlay per potential customer? Relative to sales, expenditure on antibiotics is among the lowest, yet surely the criterion in this case should be outlay per potential prescriber, since for each submarket the communications job to be done — reaching 26,000 general practitioners — is identical. On the other hand, advertising per potential customer can be extremely high in the costly capital goods industries, but, relative to sales (assuming that success is achieved), advertising expenditure will be very small indeed.

8 An Optimum Supply–Demand Equilibrium?

The threads of the discussion so far will now be drawn together. The implications for the policy maker will be examined and an evaluation of possible courses of action will be made.

The demand for advertising was seen to vary in eighteen different ways (Table 6.1). The analysis as presented, however, had two major defects. First, although *a priori* it facilitated prediction of the *direction* of a change in demand, it was incapable of predicting the *magnitude* of such a change. While upper and lower limits to the demand for advertising could sometimes be set, the optimum proved to be an elusive concept. Secondly, the analysis provided only indeterminate solutions as to the level of demand for costly or non-costly advertising styles.

Since advertising is supplied at a zero price it was suggested that consumers may demand more than they would need for optimal purchase decisions. But it is the advertiser alone who *actively* decides how much advertising will be supplied, not, as in traditional theory, the equal interaction of both suppliers and demanders in the market-place.

The possible effects of these conditions on the level of advertising actually provided can be illustrated by the supply—demand curves of Fig. 8.1. (This diagram uses conventional price—quantity axes, rather than the rod and disc analysis of Chapter 6. For the purpose a single-quantity dimension is adequate.) A perfect market is assumed. This is an assumption which will be relaxed as the discussion progresses.

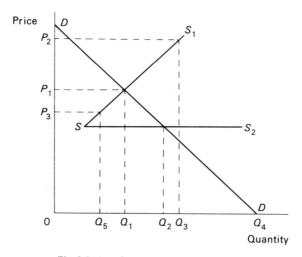

Fig. 8.1. *Supply and demand of advertising.*

DD is the demand curve for advertising. Its position and shape are determined by the various parameters discussed at length in Chapter 6. Q_4 is the quantity of advertising which will be demanded at a nil price. Q_4 will be finite because the limit to the demand for any commodity is reached when its marginal utility ultimately decreases to zero. (Moreover, the quantity demanded will in fact be somewhat less than Q_4 even at a zero price. The importance of time, as Becker points out, (1) must not be overlooked in estimating consumer demand for a product. Time which could be used to obtain other satisfactions must be given up if advertisements are to be consumed or perused. This 'cost' ensures that no commodity is demanded to the limit even at zero price.)

SS_1 is the supply curve for advertising, rising from left to right, as the costs of increasing the quantity supplied rise. SS_2 is also a cost-related supply curve but takes the shape which would be expected if costs remain stable or fall with increased output.

$P_1 Q_1$ is the price—quantity combination which would clear the market if DD and SS_1 were the relevant curves. This would be the socially optimum level of advertising. Q_2 is the comparable output level for SS_2.

The quantity of advertising supplied, however, is not determined by the market-place in this way, but rather by the sum of managerial decisions in advertising firms. It might, for example, be Q_3. This represents an excess supply — in terms of the optimum — of $Q_1 Q_3$, and a deficiency in supply — in terms of what the market will willingly absorb at zero price — of $Q_3 Q_4$. The necessary price, P_2, to ensure a quantity supplied of Q_3 is recovered in the cost of the advertised products. Equally, management might produce a quantity of advertising *below* the optimum, for example, Q_5.

Reasons why advertisers are unlikely to take decisions leading to a quantity supplied of Q_1 lie in departures from the perfectly competitive norm. These have already been discussed in Chapters 4 and 7. First, there is imperfect information in the market for advertising. The tools available to set and allocate advertising budgets fall some way short of precision in operation. Second, many advertisers are engaged in the non-perfect competition characteristic of modern industry. Several reasons were put forward as to why this phenomenon might be associated with advertising at a higher rather than a lower level than optimal.

In addition to concern over the level of advertising, considerable attention has also been paid to its moral aspects. Chapter 2 highlighted those areas where debate has been prominent, for example, over questions of truthfulness, taste, dependence of the media, and over whether advertising destroys or complements consumer sovereignty.

The economist faced with a market which is, or is alleged to be, imperfect will generally respond by recommending policies which will improve, and/or be seen to improve, the workings of that market. Such recommendations might include:

1. The making of specific references to the Monopolies Commission.
2. Imposing a tax on advertising.
3. Encouraging self-discipline by the advertising industry.
4. Passing legislation to provide direct control over advertising activity.
5. Increasing the flow of information to consumers to encourage discernment in both the purchasing of products and the 'consumption' of advertisements.
6. Raising the level of management education so that only the most sophisticated and/or least wasteful of decision tools are employed.

The first five of these points will now be examined. The sixth has been discussed in Chapter 5.

1. Use of the Monopolies Commission
The reference of specific cases to the Monopolies Commission has the virtue that there is no prior presumption made about the adequacy or inadequacy of competition in terms of the public interest. It is the Commission's job to ascertain whether or not the public interest is being served by the existing pattern of market behaviour, including advertising.

The major example of a Monopolies Commission investigation relating to advertising was the report published in 1966 on household detergents. (2) Ostensibly, Unilever and Proctor and Gamble were referred to the Commission because their respective market shares of 44 per cent and 46 per cent exceeded the statutory 33 per cent above which references can be made. The Commission found that neither market share, as such, operated against the public interest, but it did condemn their levels of advertising and promotional expenditures. The Commission went on to recommend that each should reduce such expenditure by 40 per cent. (3) This would have two effects. It would, firstly, make it easier for a small firm to enter the market, since it would not be subject to the restriction, nor would it have to meet such a high expenditure threshold to compete with the two large companies as it would have had to prior to the imposition of the restriction. Secondly, the restriction would cut the cost of the excessive advertising to Unilever and Proctor and Gamble and so enable them to compete more readily by reducing their prices to the housewife. (4)

Use of the Monopolies Commission to carry out detailed, case by case studies, and to make recommendations thereon, provides valuable insights and information on situations where, previously, relative ignorance existed. On the other hand, to treat its conclusions as revealed truth may also be misleading. For example, the Commission's recommendation of a reduction of 40 per cent in selling expenditure, which would lead to both lower entry barriers and lower prices, contains at least a degree of internal inconsistency. Reference to Fig. 7.3c shows how price can be lowered from $L + m$ to L, and how, although advertising is reduced, L becomes the entry-deterring price while output remains constant on isoquant 3.

Polanyi's study of the detergent industry came to somewhat different conclusions from those of the Monopolies Commission. He suggested, *inter alia*, that the high levels of selling costs present in the industry reflected not so much a restriction on competition but, in part, the low level of brand loyalty in the industry, coupled with a need to modify this low loyalty in order to gain the assured throughput which the industry's economies of scale in manufacturing require. He writes, 'if this objective were in practice consistently not achieved the companies would soon stop unprofitable expenditure on sales promotion'. (5)

This argument has a large degree of truth in it and is consistent with the facts of the situation. One feels, however, that Polanyi claims overmuch from empirical evidence on consumer loyalty and scale economies, and so tends to understress the impact on advertising levels of duopolistic market behaviour coupled with imperfect profit-maximising criteria for advertising decisions.

Polanyi's argument that detergent industry selling costs are not a major barrier to new competition is more attractive when he compares the powder and liquid detergent submarkets. Despite the fact that the Monopolies Commission discovered that the proportion of advertising and promotion expenditure to sales by Unilever in the liquid market was *higher* than in the powder market, the 'big two' held only 66% of that market (in 1964) compared with 96 per cent of the powder market. (6) This observation does not fit in with the Monopolies Commission diagnosis of *advertising* as an entry barrier in the detergent industry. The Commission noted that liquid detergents were an 'exception' to their hypothesis. Unfortunately they did not explain why they felt this 'exception' existed. (7)

Polanyi explains this on the grounds that manufacturing scale economies are relatively insignificant in liquids *vis-à-vis* powders, and goes on to conclude that it is these scale economies, not advertising levels, which are the major entry barrier to the powders market. Moreover, as so often happens, the paradox of advertising *aiding* entry is also present in the liquids market. Unilever, whose liquid 'Quix' was the brand leader in the early fifties, found its position dramatically undermined, on the one hand, by the Domestos product 'Sqezy' — whose revolutionary plastic container, coupled with advertising to aid product diffusion, made this the leading product of the late fifties — and on the other hand, by cheaper, relatively less sophisticated products produced by small local companies using advertising and sales promotion on a local scale to inform customers of their price advantage.

The debate on the level and quality of detergent advertising will no doubt continue. The above discussion has not been intended to illustrate the competitive effects of detergent advertising, but rather, the advantages and disadvantages of using the Monopolies Commission to pass judgement on these effects. The Commission can bring to this sort of problem a high level of analytic expertise and an alleged desire to determine what is in the public interest. It cannot, however, guarantee to provide an unambiguous and non-challengeable diagnosis of any imperfections in the market for advertising.

2. A Tax on Advertising

When the Monopolies Commission begins an investigation, it does so — at least explicitly — with no preconceptions as to the findings and recommendations it will reach. Those who advocate a tax on advertising, however, have implicitly or explicitly already accepted that the market in advertising is imperfect. In advocating taxation they are merely stating their preferred method of modifying such imperfections in order to attain an advertising quantity—quality combination which is nearer the social optimum.

In one sense, of course, the economic theorist can readily agree with those who advocate taxation. Up to a point, advertising expenditure is incurred today with a view to receiving the benefits of increased profits tomorrow. In so far as advertising is carried out in order to create goodwill rather than to obtain an instantaneous sales response it should be regarded as capital, not revenue, expenditure. However, in the preparation of company accounts for both management control and corporation tax purposes, advertising is treated as a deduction from profits before tax. It is regarded as a tax-free item of current expenditure.* If advertising were treated in common with other items of capital expenditure it would not be a tax-deductible expense appearing in the profit and loss account, but would appear as a capital asset in the firm's balance sheet.

The reasons why this treatment of advertising costs is not put into practice probably lies more in the impracticability of the bookkeeping involved than in any faults in the logic of the argument itself. For example, by no means all advertising will have an effect outwith the financial tax year in which it is incurred. The difficulty of laying down ground rules for allocating expenditures between revenue and capital accounts for the myriad variety of advertising campaigns is obvious. Even if such an allocation could be made, at what rate should the capital asset created by advertising be depreciated in the books? Should there be different depreciation rates for different campaigns with different objectives?

*This is an anomalous position which advertising expenditure shares with Research and Development outlay, which is also a cost directed at obtaining delayed rather than simultaneous benefits.

Generally, however, when a tax on advertising is advocated, people are concerned more with imposing penalties than with removing anomalies. The Labour Party in an Opposition Green Paper claim that advertising is 'subsidised by the State' (8) with, 'in effect a tax relief on advertising expenditure of about 40 per cent'. (9) Although corporation tax is around 40 per cent, and although advertising is written off in the year the expenditure is incurred, it is a little misleading to allege that a substantial subsidy is being provided as a result. If advertising were treated as a capital outlay, which within limits it should be, then, as with other capital expenditure it would be deductible from pre-tax profits in subsequent years by means of the system of capital allowances laid down in the Finance Acts. Any 'subsidy' which firms receive from the state for advertising expenditure takes the form merely of an ability to write it off in one year rather than over two or more. This is undoubtedly a financial advantage, but not a substantial one. Moreover, one wonders how some critics would react if removal of the capital–current expenditure anomaly was taken to its logical conclusion, with advertising receiving capital grants and allowances in line with the government's regional policy of the day.

In the final analysis the case for a tax on advertising rests on three propositions: that the market in advertising is imperfect; as a result, the social benefits it produces are less than the private benefits; and that a tax is the best way to remedy the situation in practice.

The first of these propositions is indisputable, and the second would seem to follow automatically. Yet does it? Few phrases are more misleading than 'perfect competition'. Few professions are less willing to modify their thinking in the light of their own acknowledged advances than are economists. It is over two decades since Schumpeter so persuasively pointed out that departures from perfect competition do more to advance than retard the consumer's standard of living. He argued that a non-perfectly competitive situation encourages 'innovation' and so, in the long run, results in more economic expansion than it discourages. As Schumpeter tritely remarked, 'cars are travelling faster . . . because they are provided with brakes'. (10) This, said Schumpeter, not perfect (price) competition is the competition which counts.

... the competition from the new commodity, the new technology, the new source of supply, the new type of organisation ... competition which commands a decisive cost or quality advantage which strikes not at the margins of profits and the output of the existing firms but at their foundations and their very lives. (11)

A fairer distribution of less is not a particularly rousing rallying call. Yet a tax on advertising in order to modify market imperfections might well result in such a situation, given that the second proposition is false (which, on a Schumpeterian rather than a Paretian analysis of society, it is).

The question one needs to ask is whether a tax is the best way to remedy advertising's undesirable aspects without forfeiting its advantages. This is the problem which needs to be attacked, not arguments leading to, or derived from, the sterile arena of the theoretical welfare economist with perfect competition as a normative goal.

In what ways might taxation be employed to reduce the quantity and/or increase the quality of advertising? Simon describes four approaches but is despairing of them as satisfactory policy instruments. 'The problem is like that in political oratory. No way has yet been found to get rid of mud-slinging without proscribing free speech.' (12) The four plans he examines are as follows:

(a) A progressively higher tax on larger levels of expenditures. Other things equal, the disadvantage of this system is that it penalises the multiproduct firm, and, possibly even more importantly, discourages new product innovation because of the higher marginal tax rate this would imply for the firm as a whole.

(b) A similar scheme could be applied to products rather than firms. While this gets over some disadvantages of the previous plan it raises more problems than it solves. Is, for example, an Austin 1300 the same product as or a different product from a Morris 1300? How would a multiproduct advert be handled? The book-keeping problems would be immense. Moreover the tax would encourage product proliferation, as firms attempted to minimise their tax bill.

(c) A third plan would be to tax most heavily those firms that spend most highly on advertising relative to their sales revenue. This would not only hit heavily at such prominent advertisers as the soap manufacturers and pharmaceutical firms, but also at less obvious scapegoats for a charge of excess advertising, such as book publishers. Furthermore such a tax might merely divert marketing resources to relatively less efficient forms of selling, such as personal salesmen.

(d) Simon argues that a flat-rate licence fee would be the 'worst of all', since its effect would be disproprotionately greater on small firms; and one might add, such a fee would reduce the liklihood of new competition, since it would raise the absolute costs of entry to an industry.

One of the most practical plans, from the viewpoint of administration, was that put forward, but never implemented, by Hugh Dalton as Chancellor of the Exchequer in 1947. His proposal was that 50 per cent of advertising expenditure, including all sales promotion, should be discriminated against by disallowing it as a deductible expense for tax purposes. The Opposition Green Paper (9) shares that view. The Green Paper suggests that such a tax would reduce the volume of advertising; by so doing 'lead to an increase in its quality', (13) 'increase the incentive for firms to seek markets by cutting prices and costs rather than by persuasive bamboozlement'; (9) and finally, raise revenue for the Exchequer of 'about £150 million per annum'. (9)

Only the first and the last of these four predictions are relatively straightforward. If advertising becomes more expensive, then certainly less of it will be undertaken, and other forms of marketing will be turned to instead. But marketing is composed of more forms of rivalry than merely price or promotional competition. Firms might, rather, turn to more intense product differentiation, or less; they might turn to costlier, more lavish, product-related services or selling environments, or the reverse. Such costs could raise costs and prices, or lower them. The effect on costs and prices would depend on the demand and cost schedules of the marketing activities chosen, and the scale of output attained, *not* necessarily on the superficial costliness or otherwise of the activity. Whether the outcome would be higher or lower prices, socially desirable or undesirable, could of course, only be assessed on the merits of the case.

Such a tax then, might, but need not, result in increased price competition. Although at first glance the suggestion has a certain plausible attraction it ignores the fact that the marketing mix is composed of more than merely advertising, selling expenditure and price rivalries. Whether or not decreasing the volume of advertising will 'lead to an increase in its quality' seems an even more contentious suggestion.* The Green Paper justifies its assertion by merely claiming that the tax would 'introduce a much needed discipline into the industry which will serve to concentrate the advertiser's mind *on his proper function*' (9) (my italics). The Green Paper does not define what this 'proper function' should be, but presumably the inference intended is that profit-maximising businessmen will be more carefully selective in their choice of advertising budgets, media and styles. This is all to the good, and greater management selectivity may help cut out excess supply of advertising in each of its three dimensions — data variety, intensity and style. There is nothing in this argument, however, to suggest that the most efficient means of advertising once selected will *not* be crude, garish, tasteless, untruthful, or whatever else might be meant by low quality.

Finally, this tax plan has several other disadvantages. Given scale economies in advertising, it again penalises disproportionately the small firm and the new entrant. This could, of course, be countered by operating some sort of sliding scale so that the full tax burden was not felt immediately a pound was spent on advertising. However, the sliding scale would have to differ industry by industry according to the entry

---

*If the objection of the writers of the Green Paper is solely to 'bamboozlement', then either legislation to correct the practice and/or extra sources of consumer information seem to be more appropriate remedies than a tax which would (necessarily) restrain the output of *all* advertising, irrespective of its quality.

barrier in each, according to the absolute and the relative levels of advertising in each, and according to the degree of both diversification and vertical integration of the firms concerned. If this tailoring of the tax to the circumstances were not done, then serious misallocation of resource flows between the sectors of the economy might result.

Moreover, the incentive to the multinational company to desist from charging 'arms-length' prices between national subsidiaries would be increased. Already, for example, Esso is under fire in the U.K. because most of its 'profits' are made by the parent company, Standard Oil of New Jersey, which charges high, non-market-determined prices to its British subsidiary. As a consequence, Esso Petroleum Ltd makes 'artificially' low profits. But it is these reported profits which are subject to corporation tax, not the 'real' level of profits concealed in the price paid to the parent company for supplies. Some Swiss pharmaceutical firms are also alleged to fail to charge 'arms-length' prices to their British subsidiaries. This tendency would be increased if advertising in Britain were to be subject to a tax of the kind suggested in the Green Paper.

The large domestic firm would also be encouraged to take advantage of favourable tax environments in this way. Advertising offices could be set up in other countries rather than remaining based in Britain. (In parallel a whole new breed of corporate tax specialists would probably also come into existence to help minimise liability to the tax.) This would further prejudice the position of the small company or the new entrant who could not afford to take such tax-evasive actions.

One objection to a tax on advertising which can be pushed to one side is that, by reducing the volume of advertising, it would prejudice the health of the media. First of all, the media could obtain, or be permitted to obtain, additional finance from other sources. Price increases for the press, or a levy on TV *manufacturers*, or pay-TV are alternatives which spring quickly to mind. This would, of course, involve some redistribution of resources in society. But the present subsidisation by TV viewers and newspaper readers probably already involves some income reallocation.

Secondly, the media might, as an alternative or complement to widening its range of income sources, reduce its expenditure levels. If advertising revenue falls so far that the colour supplements are no longer viable, would this be a great loss? (If so, of course, there is no reason why they need to be given away 'free'.) If the TV companies can produce fewer high-budget programmes, does this imply that the quality or quantity of TV output must fall? Certainly many of the best cinema films are *not* the high-budget epics. A restriction on the commercial TV companies' budgets, of course, could have a deleterious effect on the level and quality of their competition with the BBC, which relies on its licence income. This contingency could be guarded against by changing the BBC's sources and/or levels of finance in a similar way.*

However, the main purpose of this discussion is not to put the media's house in order but to emphasise that media problems need not be confused with issues relating to advertising.

A tax on advertising, then, can be used to help improve the workings of the market in advertising. It is, however, by no means a perfect instrument for this purpose.

Taplin summarised some of the main reservations about a tax on advertising, as follows:

What the consumer likes, within reason and without slumps, is price competition. So what is that same consumer going to say to a new alternative which is neither competitive advertising at its present level *nor* price cuts, but less advertising without a reduction in prices but with

---

*That competition in broadcasting is desirable is undeniable. The failure of BBC TV to introduce moving pictures into their news bulletins until *after* the advent of ITN is a clear example of the benefits of rivalry. Moreover, the cavalier attitude a semimonopoly can take when it is not immediately responsible to its sponsors for viewer satisfaction (as ITB companies must be to retain advertisements) was well illustrated during the 1972 Olympic Games. BBC screened 85 hours a week from Munich on the main channel, BBC 1, as much as the entire normal output of the channel. If you were one of the 25 per cent who did not have BBC 2, or the 90 per cent who never watch it, then, said Paul Fox, controller of BBC 1, 'there is always ITV'. (14) Regular watchers of plays, series and most documentaries and current affairs programmes had to do without. ITV, on the other hand, restricted itself to the lower-budget, better-balanced figure of 17 hours.

more taxation? It is conceivable that the consumer may not like it even although he is given assurances that the State will spend the money more wisely than industry or the consumers could have done, or that the institution of this new tax might lead to the reduction of the old ones. This argument naturally does not exhaust the discussion of the whole question of the taxation of advertising. To do that we should have to consider whether such taxation would enable freedom, range, and variety of choice by the consumers to be maintained, how the introduction of new products would be affected, and how a tax on advertisements would compare, in the light of the normal tests of the efficiency of taxes, with available alternatives. (15)

Table 8.1. *Complaints from external sources to the Advertising Standards Authority, 1971*

Result of complaint

Advertisements amended or withdrawn	20
Advertisements suspended	5
Complaints not substantiated	22
Complaints withdrawn or not proceeded with	1
Complaints satisfied with delivery of goods or refund of money	64
Mistakes by advertiser; corrective action taken	5
Satisfactory explanation given by advertiser	1
Outside purview of the Authority	2
No trace of advertiser	1
Advertiser no longer trading; complaints referred to liquidator	56*
Warnings	13
	190

Nature of complaint

Misleading claims, offers or descriptions	29
Inaccurate price claims or comparisons	1
Unsatisfactory guarantee or operation of guarantee	5
Mail order infringements	118*
Advertisement in editorial style	1
Premium offers	6
Matters of taste	20
Competitions	1
Faulty administration	2
Faulty goods or services	2
Miscellaneous breaches of other paragraphs of the Code	5
*41 relate to one company.	190

Source: Annual Report (Advertising Standards Authority, 1972).

3. Self-discipline by the Advertising Industry

An alternative to either a Monopolies Commission reference or a tax is to rely on self-control to restrict the quantity and quality of advertising to levels nearer the social optimum.

The most well-known form of voluntary control has now been in existence for over ten years. This takes the form of the Advertising Standards Authority, a body which was set up in 1962 as a result of a resolution passed at the Advertising Association's 1961 conference.

The Authority is chaired by Lord Tweedsmuir and is currently composed of eight other individuals, none of whom officially represent any particular vested interest. Only two of the eight have any overt connection with advertising, and are managing directors of media firms rather than advertising agencies. The remaining members of the Authority include the Director of Education and Training of the CBI, the Assistant General Secretary of the TUC, the Chairman of the Women's Group on Public Welfare and a former headmistress of Roedean School.

Any member of the public can complain to the Authority about any advertisement. All that is required is a letter of explanation and a copy of the advert to which exception was taken. The bulk of the Authority's work lies in supervising the British Code of Advertising Practice and investigating complaints from the public about adverts which allegedly breach the Code's standards.*

Table 8.1 gives a breakdown of cases investigated by the ASA arising from external complaints in 1971. More than half of all complaints arose from the failure of mail order advertisers either to supply goods or to refund money. A substantial number of complainants received satisfaction, but in one case the ASA had no alternative but to pass on forty-one claims to the liquidator of the bankrupt firm. The only other two types of complaint to exceed double figures were those relating to matters of taste and misleading copy. One advertiser, for example, wished to promote his hairdryer by using the photograph of a notorious criminal showing off

---

*The 4th, 1972, edition of the code is reproduced in the Appendix, together with the list of organisations who support the Code.

six different hair styles. The Authority took the stance that
the fact that the man was a criminal did not warrant
relaxation of the Code's rule that his permission must be
obtained before he could be portrayed in an advert. The
proportion of complaints relating to misleading claims has
been steadily declining over the years. One, which was
challenged by the ASA and immediately dropped, was made
by a central-heating manufacturer. The comparative statistics
on running costs that the firm was alleging were wholly
inconsistent with what is regarded, by all major fuel interests,
as the established pattern of costs for various fuels.

There is little to complain of, and much to commend, in
the work of the Advertising Standards Authority and the
Code of Advertising Practice. Their existence no doubt
dampens the potential excesses of irresponsible advertisers.
However, the Authority cannot, by its very nature as an
offshoot of the industry itself, be wholly objective. For
example, the industry may be tempted to use the Authority
as an instrument to dampen the excesses of irresponsible
critics. As such, this may be no bad thing, but the dangers of
such a conflict of interests within the same body do not
make for confidence that it will ensure a socially optimal
advertising level and content.

4. Legislation

While there are a large number of Acts designed to protect
the interests of consumers, none of these are solely and
exclusively concerned with advertising. Those Acts which
most specifically encroach upon the advertiser's freedom of
movement include the Merchandise Marks Act, 1887–1953;
the Sale of Goods Act, 1893; the Consumer Protection Act,
1961; the Misrepresentation Act, 1966; the Trade Descriptions
Act, 1968; and the Fair Trading Act, 1973. The Misrepresentation Act enables consumers to sue for damages if they have
been the victims of fraud or misleading statements resulting in
the purchase of worthless products. Fraud or misleading
statements are an offence under the Trade Descriptions Act.

Specific legislation to control advertising is, then, not
particularly overt in Britain. What there is of it is desirable
and unobjectionable from the viewpoint of the individual

consumer in whose interests it is meant to operate. The question which requires an answer, however, is whether or not any extension of this legislation is required to bring the supply of advertising closer to its social optimum in both nature and extent?

To answer this question, specific pieces of legislation — actual or proposed — must be examined, and judged on their merits. Comparison with the laws of other nations may be useful. For example, Sweden has recently introduced a Consumer Ombudsman. He will work along side the Ombudsman, who has long existed to protect the Swedish public against bureaucratic abuses of the Civil Service.

The Consumer Ombudsman will receive complaints from the public about unfair trade practices and deceptive advertisements, and will also keep his eyes on the market by reading newspapers and magazines. In minor cases he is entitled to forbid a company to run a certain advertisement on pain of a fine, and in more important cases he can bring the culprits before the Market Court, which consists of representatives for the producers, for the consumers, and impartial judges. So far, nothing very spectacular has occurred in this field, except that the Consumer Ombudsman has got far more mail than he has time to read. But some injunctions have already been issued, and advertisers are certainly increasingly sensitive to the risk of a fine.

However, nothing has happened yet to a piece of tourist propaganda that was seriously considered to be misleading in a pilot study made in connection with the preparation of the new law. This was an advertisement saying, 'Come to Oslo, the City for Fun'. Now, everybody who has seen the place knows that the capital of Norway is not a City for Fun, so the pilot study concluded that this was a case of reprehensible misinformation. (16)

A Consumer Ombudsman certainly has much to commend him. Unlike the Advertising Standards Authority, he would not be subject to, or suspect of, divided loyalties. He would share, in common with methods of voluntary restraint, the advantages of *not* being rigidly bound by statute law, but would be able to build up his position on the basis of precedent and case law. Such an accretion of precedent over time would provide opportunities for flexibility in interpretation on matters of taste, professional etiquette and so on, where statutory rules can become irrelevant or impracticable with the passing of the years.

Although it is still early to judge, similar advantages of flexibility seem to be built into the 1973 Fair Trading Act. This provides for the setting up of a Consumer Protection Advisory Committee. The CPAC will study 'consumer trade practices' (defined so as to include advertising) to ascertain whether they adversely affect consumers' economic interests. Referrals to the CPAC can be made by the Director General of Fair Trading of any advert which he considers, for example, to be misleading, to withhold adequate information, or is confusing. The CPAC in its report can make recommendations that the 'practice' be amended or withdrawn. The Secretary can, in turn, lay down a statutory instrument to give effect to the recommendations or modified versions of them.

This picture of an independent, objective tribunal receives something of a jolt, however, when one turns to a country with a much longer history of advertising restriction, the United States. The most potent regulations are contained in the Federal Trade Commission Act of 1914. The Commission was established to stop unfair competition, and in 1938 the Wheeler-Lea amendments redefined 'unfair methods of competition' to specifically include 'deceptive acts or practices'.

Over the years the FTC has performed a large amount of diligent work, culminating in 1965 with the adoption of a rule which would require cigarette firms to include in their adverts a warning that smoking might be dangerous. (Congress later passed a law requiring such a message on the packet, but not in the advertisement.)

More recently, however, a considerable amount of concern has been expressed about the FTC's activities, not only in advertising, but also in academic circles. The FTC can unilaterally declare that any particular advertisement is deceptive, and the burden of proving innocence is left to the advertiser. This system is not only the obverse of normal judicial arrangements, whereby an accused is regarded as innocent until proved guilty, but, by publicising the presumed guilt, must harm the advertiser's goodwill and make it very hard indeed for the smaller firm to raise the resources, from its now depleted revenue, to finance a defence.

Professor Brozen (17) cites one case which has achieved a degree of notoriety. This was the judgement made against the ITT subsidiary, Continental Baking, and its adverts for Wonder Bread. 'The FTC claimed, that by emphasising Wonder Bread's nutritive value the company is *implying* its product is unique when, in fact, other enriched loaves have the same nutritive value. The FTC has not claimed that the advertisements are false, nor that they misrepresent the product. They simply say that what was claimed was not unique.'

This case highlights the dangers which exist if overenthusiastic administrators are charged with interpreting and invoking an already extant and apparently acceptable code of laws. The surprising inference must be made that the FTC is 'insisting that an advertiser provide no information concerning his product if some other products have the same virtues. Only if he proclaims that other products do what his does can he advertise the virtues of the product'. (17) Continental intends to fight this judgement, 'to the Supreme Court if necessary'. Certainly Continental's stance must attract a large element of sympathy. If the FTC judgement is upheld, advertisements will either have to contain minimal product information, or so much data qualifying the claims made in comparison with competing products that the consumer will either end up with an inadequate supply of information relative to demand, or a supply that is so complete, but so full of small-print provisos, that he will turn away in confusion. Moreover the cost of collecting comparative information for inclusion in adverts would certainly be above zero, and so, other things equal, expenditure on advertising would rise significantly. Again this would have a deleterious effect on the small firm already finding difficulty in meeting advertising expenditure thresholds.

That a benevolent legislature could pass far-sighted laws which directed the quantity and quality of advertising to precisely the optimum point is, of course, an attractive notion. The myriad variables which would have to be taken into consideration, however, would put the conception of such legislation beyond the reach of even a battery of powerful computers. The impracticability of such an 'ultimate and ideal law', however, should not discourage discussion on three vital areas of social concern.

First, laws can play a big part in protecting the consumer from dishonest and untruthful statements. Can such legislation be improved or extended? Second, laws can modify or prohibit advertising of socially undesirable products. (Thus cigarette advertisements must contain a health warning, and further, they are currently not permitted at all on TV. Also, both the consumption and advertising of narcotic drugs is prohibited outright.) Whether or not scope for improvement exists here can only be decided on the basis of product by product studies.

The third point is more controversial but, if anything, more fundamental. This is the desire of certain people to use the rule of law to direct advertising and consumer choice when individual consumers themselves would not wish to be so influenced, and to do so over an array of products far wider in extent than merely those (such as cigarettes) which a concensus view might regard as being prejudicial to individual health or social well-being. All laws impinge on individual freedom. At times this is no bad thing. In even the freest of societies, the freedom one man has to move his fist is limited to the proximity of the other fellow's chin. At other times increasing the framework of laws does more to diminish responsible freedom than to enhance it. How can one begin to decide when this point is reached?

In the market for advertising, one should ask two questions. First, who loses most from poor advertising decisions? The answer is twofold. The advertiser may over- or underspend if he misjudges the market. As a result the consumer may make a suboptimal purchase, for example, by buying the 'wrong' article or paying too much for the 'right' one. There is certainly a loss to society involved if advertisers make wrong decisions. But the loss is borne by the advertiser, through lower earnings, and/or the consumer, through lower utility per pound spent.*

The second question to be asked is: Who has the information to make advertising decisions which will be closest to optimal? The answer again is twofold, the suppliers and demanders of advertising, those most intimately involved with the decision. The advertiser, as a result of market study, knows most accurately the type and nature of advertisement most required by the market segment at which he is aiming. The consumer of the product advertised knows most precisely the sort of product information he wants before he will make a purchase decision in the light of the range of other expenditure alternatives facing him.

In other words, it is the members of the market in advertising, consumers and producers, who have the most to lose from poor decisions and, therefore, who have the greatest incentive to take correct decisions relating to the production and consumption of advertisements. It is these same consumers and producers who know most about the decision situation they are involved in; it is they, therefore, who have the greatest ability to take correct advertising decision.

Under these circumstances is it probable that legislators, however benevolent, know best? They have neither the incentive nor the ability to know what producers and consumers desire in their own best interests. Furthermore it would be naive to assume that legislators always are, or even frequently are, benevolent. Legislation can too often be partisan in origin, or smack of a self-righteousness on the part of the legislator, which has little in common with the self-interest of those the legislation nominally exists to protect or guide.

Few things can be more presumptive, or insulting to the freedom of the individual than a belief that the State knows best. Few things can be more socially *élitist* than a refusal to allow the individual to act as he wishes. Yet this is the road

---

*This ignores losses to the government in the form of lower corporation tax receipts, and any monopoly distortions associated with the advertiser's decisions.

down which legislation tends to travel. The Swedish Government is currently considering establishing a consumer agency which explicitly will *not* accept the values of the consumer, but will try to influence them. Tarschys cites from the Government Report proposing the agency:

> When appraising the household's needs one cannot — as a foundation for the activities of the Agency — rely to any conclusive degree on the consumers' pretensions, expressed through the demand for products and in another manner. It is a well-known fact that in many respects, in matters of diet for example, these pretensions can be altogether too modest. As in other public sectors the needs here must be formulated in terms of norms based on the community's ambitions regarding the well-being of the individual. [*Konsumantpolitik* SOU (1971) 28.]

In effect, Tarschys says, the legislators have adopted an attitude of 'damn the consumer and let's get down to business — let's decide ourselves what he should really demand and reform the market from above.' (18)

5. More Sources of Consumer Information
The market in advertising is imperfect. Legislation and taxation are, at best, removers of the symptoms of imperfection. At worst they remove the freedom of the individual to select, experience and reject, and so, in the last analysis, they inhibit the innovative activity which can provide the multiplicity of goods and services which alone, by their sheer variety, can satisfy the myriad wants of a diverse population.* The Monopolies Commission is more of a diagnostic tool than a prescriptive instrument, while voluntary restraint by the advertising industry must always be susceptible to some degree of bias.

There remains the possibility of attempting to remove the market imperfections themselves. Ways of doing this on the

---

*Some consumers may on occasion, prefer idleness to earning in order to be able to consume. Only innovative activity, however, in the form of more efficient ways of doing things, can result in maintained earnings *and* increased leisure.

supply side of the market have been discussed at length in Chapters 4 and 5. But even if managerial decision taking could be perfected, this would only enable advertisers to keep their activities close to a private, rather than a social optimum. Because of its zero price an excessive amount of advertising would still be provided. Because of its source (the seller) it would still contain degrees of special pleading. Moreover, as the Economists' Advisory Group pointed out, (19) the laws of libel ensure that competitors' advertising cannot draw attention to weak points in rival's products: points which will inevitably have been ignored in the rival's adverts.

The EAG argue two further propositions from this set of circumstances. First, although advertising information is provided 'free', contrary to normal theory, this does not mean that the level supplied will be excessive. The costs of providing a system of advertising information dissemination ('contract costs') whereby the advertising could be charged for in the market-place, rather than supplied 'free' as a joint product with the advertised good, might well be more than the social costs involved in having advertising at its current level of provision.

> The fact that advertising continues to be supplied over a very wide range of commodities by a very large number of suppliers, and over a long period of time, suggests *a priori* that it is the cheapest way of supplying that kind of information. If that were not so, it would be reasonable to expect firms to be established that would specialise in the production of that information for profit. (20)

This is a valid argument, but one could retort that the costs of policing a price system for advertising information would be so great as to render it well-nigh impracticable.* So great, in fact, that conventional advertising levels could rise considerably higher than they already are without exceeding such costs, and therefore without being excessive in the sense

---

*See pp. 76–77 for an explanation as to why the introduction of the price system into the market for advertising information would be so costly.

of the EAG's argument. Conversely, while existing advertising levels may not be excessive in this sense, they may still be some unknown quantity above the level needed by consumers to make optimal purchase decisions. The second inference that the EAG draw is also well grounded in theory but, in terms of applicability, is a much firmer proposition on which to build a policy decision. That is, to offset the inevitable bias in advertising and its lack of contradiction, there should be some additional and independent information source.

The need for *alternative* information is self-evident, for *additional* it is less so. The case for additional information rests on the fact that information is a public good, and as a result the private benefits which producers of information would be able to recoup through the market-place would be less than the social benefits which information provides. Consequently, less information will be produced than is optimal, and therefore a recommendation for additional information can be made.

This is certainly logically correct but it ignores the fact that advertising is a type of information which has evolved to overcome the shortfall which must exist if the market-place alone is left to supply the public good of information. Advertising information levels may equal, exceed or fall short of optimal information levels. In so far as they fall short, additional information is obviously required. In so far as they exceed it, additional information is required *only* because the *mix* of total advertising information supplied in the three dimensions of data variety, intensity or style is in imbalance relative to consumer need. Because of the source of advertising information this imbalance must exist, and therefore the consumer requires additional information.

It is easy, therefore, to agree with the EAG that consumers have 'too little independent information in particular'. Given that information is not a homogeneous commodity one cannot so readily agree, however, that 'consumers have too little information in general'. (21) The only generalisation which can be made is that advertising information may, but need not, be in excess of consumer need, but inevitably the mix of that information, whether excessive or deficient in total, will be suboptimal, and as a result additional independent information is required to offset bias and to remedy particular, if not general, information deficiencies.

There is, of course, already an excellent consumer information service provided by the Consumers' Association and its magazine *Which*. The organisation has a paying membership of over half-a-million people, and *Which* has a readership considerably in excess of this figure. These facts are at once encouraging and discouraging. The influence of *Which* is understated by the number of subscribers. Yet this illustrates again the difficulties of producing and selling information in a fashion which enables sufficient revenue to be recouped to render the operation viable.

The Consumers' Association, however, is open to criticism on three fronts. One of these criticisms is frequently heard, two much less often.

First, it is often alleged that the Consumers' Association has no influence on the mass market and therefore on consumer decisions, and so, in turn, on corporate product policy and advertising decisions. This is the view taken by the Opposition Green Paper when they say that 'the consumer movement is predominantly middle class and intellectual and that, although all consumers are equal, some are more equal than others'. (22) The 'sophisticated' middle-class consumer and CA member is presumed, in any event, to be in less need of the information services of the CA. The best response to this criticism, however, is contained in a recent comment in *Which*:

> The weary old reproach that *Which* and CA are hopelessly middle class is now out of date. Anyone who makes it does not know what is going on.
> First the *Daily Mirror*. It was their idea. They wanted value-for-money information for their readers — facts which would help them to know all about HP rates and credit arrangements, about the possible dangers from frozen chickens, about how people manage the family budget. They asked us to supply the research (for which they paid) and they supplied the journalism. The result is that *Which* type information is now reaching the 10 million readers of the *Daily Mirror*. (23)

The same issue of *Which* contained details of a Consumer Advice Centre in Kentish Town which the CA had set up on an experimental basis. It was tailored for those who prefer to get shopping advice by word of mouth, and not by reading. As a result of the experiment's success, Harlow, Havering and Greenwich Local Authorities are emulating the venture. They are either paying CA to run the Centres in total, or are paying the CA for the information and running the Centres independently.

So the CA's influence is undoubtedly more broadly based than the Opposition Green Paper gives it credit for. Moreover, the breakthrough with the *Daily Mirror* could set up something of a virtuous circle in the newspaper world. It is the papers with highest circulations which attract the most advertising. It is the papers which provide what their readers (i.e. consumers) want who get these mass circulations. If consumer information in the press from an independent source is attractive to readers, then mass circulation consumer information in a financially healthy press will be the outcome. And this information would be lying cheek by jowl with advertisements, thus providing yet another constraint for over enthusiastic advertisers to work within.

The remaining two criticisms of the CA are less frequently voiced. One is that, given a shortage of objective information on products, the CA should concentrate its scarce resources on those areas where the need is greatest, for example, on expensive, rather than low-cost products, on infrequently purchased items rather than everyday items. It is in these areas that the risk of loss to a consumer is greatest, and in these cases that the consumer cannot gain information cheaply through experience, and so the need for information to lessen such risks is highest. Thus the CA should concentrate on stereograms rather than marmalade, on cars rather than washing powders. This topic has already been discussed in detail in Chapter 6 and summarised in Table 6.1.

The third cricitism of the CA is that it is a monopoly supplier. Of course, there are substitutes for its 'products' in the form of advertising and word-of-mouth product data from existing users of advertised products. But it is because of the inadequacy of these substitutes that the CA is required. The dangers of a single source of independent information becoming the mouthpiece of one pressure group or another are too obvious to require elaboration here. The CA already has a deservedly high reputation for objectivity. In a monopoly situation, if this objectivity were to vanish, then the consumers' interest would be damaged. In a situation of rivalry the liklihood of the same direction of bias from all sources of information would be less. If it is accepted that additional independent information is required, then this requirement could be met by establishing some sort of rival to the CA which would simultaneously meet the critisicm of the CA being a monopoly.

This raises the question of how such a rival body would be financed. Generally, when the provision of a good or service results in large-scale external benefits which cannot be recouped in the market-place, the response is to recommend State provision. (The lighthouse service is the classic textbook example of a service which no private firm could provide, unless the lighthouse keepers had exceptionally long arms to reach out for fees to ships passing in the night!) The commodity of consumer information would also appear to be typical of such a commodity and, indeed, we have argued so at various places in this work.

However, there are several reasons why State provision of consumer information should be regarded as unnecessary or even undesirable. First, leaving an information service in the hands of the State provides the opportunity, if no more, of misuse by the government of the day. The road to 1984 is paved with good intentions. This is one reason why the proposal of a National Consumer's Authority, as proposed by the Opposition Green Paper, should be rejected. The Authority would be 'on the lines of the American FTC' (*sic*) and would have resources for comparative testing of products, would be responsible for the general surveillance of all advertisements, and would publicise its results. (24)

A second reason for rejecting State provision of information is that, if provided free of charge, it would rapidly push privately funded bodies such as the CA out of existence.

Thirdly, many arguments in favour of public provision of

services when external economies exist ignore the possibilities of 'internalising' the conditions in question into normal buyer—seller relationships. The costs involved in internalising such conditions may be far less than the external detriments of public provision, which include the administrative tendency for top-heavy overcentralisation, resistance to change, susceptibility to political pressures, and the opportunity cost of the rivalry foregone, with its impulse for cost reduction, quality variation and innovation. Internalising such costs would seem relatively easy here when so much independent consumer information is already provided in the marketplace. The CA already exists. Rivalry in the provision of information about restaurants and hotels already takes place very extensively. (The CA produces the *Good Food Guide*, Dunlop Ltd, the 'Egon Ronay' guide, and the two motoring organisations produce similar, less extensive, but longer established handbooks of information.)

How then might a rival, non-nationalised consumer information service be set up and financed? One way would be for the State to approve a second body and subsidise it *and* the CA on an equal footing. This would both minimise (but not avoid) the dangers of political pressures on such a body, while maintaining rivalry in the provision of information. Alternatively another body might set itself up, with the assistance of the media, in much the same way as the CA is being aided by the *Daily Mirror*. The trades union movement might set up such an organisation, and finance its running costs by sales of publications, or even by a levy on its members. Co-operative Societies might be even more apposite movers in this field given their traditional role as protectors of consumer interests.

The methods are legion but it is beyond the scope of this work to go further. Certainly, independent information is in inadequate supply, but equally certainly, if we fail as a community to fill this deficiency, the fault will lie with ourselves, not with our political masters.*

*The Minister for Trade and Consumer Affairs has already announced his wish for a nationwide chain of consumer advice centres supported by the Department of Trade and Industry. (25)

9 Concluding Thoughts

'Contrariwise,' continued Tweedledee,
'if it was so, it might be; and if it
were so, it would be: but as it isn't,
it ain't. That's logic.'
Lewis Carroll

The subject of advertising does not lend itself to the making of neat and definitive conclusions. To avoid the presumption which is implicit in a conclusion, this chapter will, rather, question some of the basic assumptions on which earlier chapters have rested. For example, the economic analysis of markets on which Chapters 6, 7 and 8 were based can be alleged to be a redundant intellectual exercise. If so, then the view already adopted that it is only the supplier of advertising, not the consumer, who *actively* decides the level at which advertising will settle is, in fact, reinforced, not contradicted. Albeit, it will be shown that this conclusion can be arrived at in a somewhat different manner. But this, too, may be challenged, and it will be argued that consumers *do* have and *do* exercise a choice between different levels of advertising consumption. If this is so, then rather than alleging that advertising may be 'too high', the counterproposition that there is 'not enough' advertising may have to be entertained.

In this upside-down manner the preceding chapters will be summarized, and scope for further investigation and discussion will be revealed.

1. Is Market Analysis Obsolete?

J. K. Galbraith's *New Industrial State* is possibly the most persuasive of all recent writings which claim that the market is merely a theoretical abstraction with little or no basis in present-day reality. (1) The 'technostructure', or decision-taking team of the modern 'mature corporation', does not, according to Galbraith, respond to the needs and wants of consumers in the market place. Consumer sovereignty is out of date. This sovereignty of the consumer allegedly ensured that firms produced what consumers wanted. The place of advertising in the scheme of things was to assist consumers to make their choices as sensibly and swiftly as possible, if the product were new, then unless the advertiser had anticipated correctly the needs of the consumer, the product and the advertising would both fail.

The technostructure, as seen by Galbraith however, does not exist to serve the consumer. It exists to perpetuate itself and to achieve 'the greatest possible rate of corporate growth as measured in sales'. This goal is readily explicable in that it increases the opportunities for promotion, prestige and pecuniary reward available to the technocrats. It can be pursued because the mature corporation no longer operates within the normal constraints of a market economy where success and failure in satisfying consumer demand are measured by the familiar yardsticks of profit and loss.

Clearly, if this is so, then market analysis by the professional economist must be relegated to the position of a harmless pastime. How does Galbraith justify his assertions? He claims that the mature corporation can free itself from the market if some, or all, of the following conditions hold:

(a) It earns sufficient (but not maximum) profits to keep existing shareholders quiescent.
(b) It earns sufficient profits for plough-back purposes to make it independent of outside sources (future shareholders) of finance.
(c) Close links with government ensure guaranteed sales, or subsidies of products provided to national agencies.
(d) Advertising and sales techniques enable the corporation to reach forward to the consumer and ensure that the

market will absorb the products which the firm makes at the price which the firm is willing to accept.

Galbraith has an attractive polemic style and his views (including his concern for the consumer and the quality of life) are widely respected. Unfortunately, empirical evidence does not support his belief that advertising can liberate the mature corporation from the market, and so dethrone the sovereign consumer. The 1966 £3.2 million loss of the British Motor Corporation can be traced to lack of an attractive product range. The Princess R and early 1800 models launched in the mid-sixties were failures. No medium-range models were introduced between the successful launch of the Mini and 1100 series in 1959 and 1961, respectively, and 1966, the year of the loss. BMC was just not producing what the customer wanted. No amount of 'reaching forward' to the consumer by advertising could have liberated the BMC technocracy from the market. The histories of the Cunard steamship company in the face of airline competition; of the British and American motor industries in the face of Japanese and European competition; of the coal industry in the face of oil and nuclear power could all be cited as examples of mature corporations where the 'technocracies' failed to meet the will of the market and, as a result, either adjusted their policies in line with demand or went under.

The consumer's interest, in fact, would appear to be less at risk when he is face to face with the mature corporation than when the corporation is face to face with the government. 'It is too easy to persuade politicians and officials whose own money is not at stake that journeys to the moon, ever more advanced aircraft or home-based computer industries should be subsidised from the public purse.' (2)

A wish to disparage the philosophy of consumer sovereignty may be due to a dislike of the materially based society which consumers have chosen.* This is an understandable stance. To claim, without evidence, that materialism is the result of technocratic advertising is less understandable. For example, in an earlier work, Galbraith wrote:

*A standpoint taken by Toynbee, op. cit., Chapter 2, p. 6.

Were it so that a man on arising each morning was assailed
by demons which instilled in him a passion sometimes for
silk shirts, sometimes for kitchenware, sometimes for
chamber-pots and sometimes for orange squash, there
would be every reason to applaud the effort to find the
goods, however odd, that quenched this flame. But should
it be that his passion was the result of his first having
cultivated the demons ... (by assimilating the output of
modern advertising and salesmanship) ... there would be
question as to how rational was his solution. (3)

The British Labour movement spent a century unashamed-
ly campaigning on a materialistic platform for redistribution
of income within society so that the previously poor could
enjoy luxuries, new experiences and amenities over and above
the essentials for living. Now that mass poverty has been
abolished, there is a tendency among some writers such as
Galbraith to disparage the materialistic benefits which mass
society has itself wanted. Material self-denial by well-heeled
Harvard professors can be a virtue; if it is practised to benefit
others then it is even more virtuous; but if preached in the
belief that self-indulgence of any kind is somehow wrong, it
can be positively selfish.

2. Does the Consumer Have Power in the Advertising Market?

Whether market analysis is obsolete or not, the conclusion of
earlier chapters was that the consumer in the advertising
market took no active part in determining the supply levels of
advertising information. The consumer was alleged to be
willing to accept advertising levels which would be well above
the optimum necessary for a purchase decision to be made.
This was argued to be the result of the intrinsic benefits (say,
in terms of pleasure or enjoyment) which advertising can
provide. So advertising can possibly exceed the optimum for
some time before negative returns set in. This, coupled with
imperfections on the supply side of the market (say, in terms
of non-availability of adequate management tools to determine the optimum), may well result in an excess supply of
advertising. It appears, therefore, that those who believe in

the utility of conventional market analysis to explain economic phenomena arrive at the same conclusion as those who believe that the market has been rendered obsolete by technocratic advertising reaching forward to the consumer. Both deduce that the level at which advertising settles is only actively taken by suppliers. Both argue that this level may be higher than necessary, albeit they arrive at this conclusion by different routes.

The charge, however, may not be wholly accurate. Consumer choice, and the power to exercise that choice and make its influence felt, may not be as insignificant a force in the advertising market as the preceding arguments tend to suggest. The ability of the consumer to choose a level of advertising is the same as the ability to choose between similar products with different levels of advertising support. This is perhaps most easily illustrated by reference to the grocery trade where the housewife can frequently choose between a nationally available manufacturer's brand and a product branded privately by the retailer.

For example, the Nielsen organisation examined all available products in ten important classes with a total sales value of £148.3 million in 1967. (4) These ten product classes received total advertising support of £6.6 million in that same year. Manufacturers' advertised brands accounted for 70.6 per cent of total sales value, but consumer preferences were such that the remaining 29.4 per cent of total sales were privately branded products. This consumer choice, however, was exercised in defiance of a disproportionately high level of advertising support to the manufacturers' brands. Manufacturers' brands received 88.7 per cent of the £6.6 million outlay on advertising; the remaining products received only 11.3 per cent of that outlay but achieved 29.4 per cent of total sales.

Clearly the consumers were influenced not only by advertising differences but also by the accompanying price differences. On average, Neilsen discovered that the private brands were 24 per cent cheaper than the heavily advertised products, and this comparison was done at the point of sale, so taking account of any price cutting by the retailer. In practice, of course, it is almost impossible to isolate the effects on the consumer's decision process of the different elements, such as price and advertising, in the marketing mix. The mix also includes the element of product quality, and this too affects decisions. (The ten product classes of the Neilsen study included liquid detergents and instant coffee, which are rarely distinguishable one brand from another; it also included squashes, and in this class, private labelled products have become notoriously poor in quality *vis-à-vis* the more expensive manufacturers' products.)

Nevertheless, provided there is active competition in an industry — either potential through new entry, or within the industry, such as in groceries, or even within a duopoly such as detergents, where the manufacturers themselves produce low-price, low-advertising budget brands — then the consumer will be able to choose the level of advertising he or she wishes to demand in the market-place. *If this choice is available*, unfettered by complications such as variable quality or reliability, *then there can be no general presumption that too much will be supplied*. As in all cases of firms inadequately responding to consumer need, advertisers indulging in oversupply would pay the penalty of forfeiture of market share to the lesser-advertised, lower-priced product.

3. Wanted: More Advertising and a New Theory of Competition?

There would appear to be two main viewpoints which the observer of advertising can adopt. He can accept, as is argued in most of the earlier chapters, that advertising is in excess supply. Or he can take the stance that consumers will reject products that are excessively advertised, and so discourage unnecessary advertising.

Regretably, we have already had to conclude in Chapters 5, 6 and 7 that there are no valid technical or other criteria for 'excessiveness'. Could it be that the search for such a criterion is merely a hunt for a will-o'-the-wisp? Should not the goal, rather, be to ascertain whether the market in advertising works efficiently? This has nothing to do with the presence or absence of perfect competition, but as in all other markets, whether or not the consumer is receiving the product he wants, in the quality, at the place, at the time and at the price he is willing to pay. If some producers are failing to meet his needs, do alternative sources of supply exist, and can they be easily tapped? 'Excessiveness', in other words, should be determined by the adequacy (not the 'perfection') of competition in meeting consumer need, rather than the other way round.

Perfect competition may have to be rejected as a model, not only because it is unrealistic but also because it is non-ideal. For example, it could be argued that the choice a consumer has between a heavily advertised brand and a non-advertised substitute is influenced by the advertising itself. If so, the choice is not completely free, and fewer people may choose to buy the non-advertised product than would have, had the heavy advertising not been present. This may be so, but if the object of competition is an adequate and efficient meeting of consumer needs, rather than the attainment of a 'perfect' state, than that object is achieved by shifting all cost curves in an industry downwards through process innovation,* rather than merely equalising them between suppliers. If this is what the consumer wants, then some degree of (non-perfectly competitive) monopoly protection to both firms and their products may be required to provide attractive profit levels, which would encourage entrepreneurs to seek for better, cheaper ways of producing existing goods, and to seek for better, more satisfying products to replace some of, or add to, the range of products already facing the consumer. One way to obtain this protection from the Schumpeterian 'gale of creative destruction' is by advertising. In other words, the analysis put forward in Chapter 7, that advertising is a departure from perfect competition, need not be an argument that advertising is in excess of the levels required for adequate competition.

If a new theory of competition is required (and some form of Schumpterian renaissance probably is needed), then it would have to incorporate the idea that there can be too

---

*And to create new production functions and new cost curves through product innovation.

little product differentiation as well as too much: that *advertising can be too low* as well as too high.*

If this book, by its very deficiencies, goes some way to encouraging others to develop a new theory of competition which will firmly locate advertising in its proper role, as an aid to competition which is adequate and efficient in satisfying consumer wants rather than 'perfect' in the traditional sense, then it will have achieved one of its principal objectives. However, like all outside inquirers into a subject, I do not doubt that both supporters and detractors of advertising as a social phenomenon will be convinced that I am biased in favour of the other.

---

*That advertising can be *below* the optimum has already been suggested in Chapter 4, Section 2b, where it was pointed out how the advent of local radio advertising will enable consumer needs and supply availability to be more closely, and less wastefully matched.

On a larger scale, it can be argued that the ban on advertising imposed by most professional bodies on their members is not in the consumers' interest. The only way a practitioner can attract new business is by personal recommendation, a method of information exchange which is not subject to the checks and balances of a publicly proclaimed advertisement. Similarly, the only way a man can set up his own practice is to work for an established firm for a time and then leave, hoping that a number of his old employer's clients will desert with him. This is not the most satisfactory of ways to encourage new entry and increased consumer choice in an industry. Yet the Institute of Chartered Accountants (to take an example) devote ten-and-a-half pages of their rule book to ensuring that its members remain as anonymous as possible. Rules are even provided about the maximum size of typeface which may be used for a firm's name when it places a press recruitment advertisement.

Not only accountants', but medical profession advertising also, could greatly assist client or patient choice of practice. Information could be included in adverts on the qualifications of practice members; the total number of patients the practice is responsible for; the provision made for private patients; whether practice members consult each other for second opinions; whether or not ancillary practice staff are employed; how frequently house calls are made; and even simple, but perhaps not widely known information on surgery hours and holidays.

Specialisation within professions would increase, as practitioners were allowed to advertise their speciality. Solicitors, for example, would be able to specialise in divorce, or conveyancing, or driving offence charges, and so on.

(Advertising restrictions by the professions have been under examination by the Monopolies Commission since May, 1973.)

Appendix

THE BRITISH CODE OF ADVERTISING PRACTICE*

The Code has the support of the following organisations whose representatives constitute the Code of Advertising Practice (CAP) Committee:

ADVERTISING ASSOCIATION
BRITISH DIRECT MAIL ADVERTISING ASSOCIATION
BRITISH POSTER ADVERTISING ASSOCIATION
DIRECT MAIL PRODUCERS ASSOCIATION
ELECTRICAL SIGN MANUFACTURERS ASSOCIATION
INCORPORATED SOCIETY OF BRITISH ADVERTISERS
INDEPENDENT TELEVISION COMPANIES ASSOCIATION
INSTITUTE OF PRACTITIONERS IN ADVERTISING
MASTER SIGN MAKERS ASSOCIATION
NEWSPAPER PUBLISHERS ASSOCIATION
NEWSPAPER SOCIETY
PERIODICAL PUBLISHERS ASSOCIATION
PROPRIETARY ASSOCIATION OF GREAT BRITAIN
SCOTTISH DAILY NEWSPAPER SOCIETY
SCOTTISH NEWSPAPER PROPRIETORS ASSOCIATION
SCREEN ADVERTISING ASSOCIATION
SOLUS OUTDOOR ADVERTISING ASSOCIATION

The Code is under the general supervision of the Advertising Standards Authority.

*Fourth edition, April 1970 (© CAP Committee 1970). A new edition was in preparation when this book went to press.

PART A

Preamble

All advertising should be legal, decent, honest and truthful.

No advertisement should bring advertising into contempt or reduce confidence in advertising as a service to industry and to the public.

The Code is to be applied in the spirit as well as the letter.

It covers all advertising of products and services. The advertising of medicines, treatments and appliances is subject to the additional provisions set out in part B.

A list of statutes affecting advertising is set out in Appendix I. Particular attention is drawn to the Trade Descriptions Act 1968.

Interpretation

1.1 The word "advertisement" throughout this Code applies to advertising wherever it may appear including advertising in leaflets, circulars and price lists and on packages, labels and point of sale material.

1.2 Any illustration included in an advertisement is subject to the same rules.

1.3 For the purpose of this Code a service is a product and is subject to the same rules.

Descriptions, Claims and Comparisons

2.1 All descriptions, claims and comparisons should be capable of substantiation, and advertisers and advertising agencies are required to provide such substantiation without delay when called upon to do so.

2.2 Advertisements should not contain any description, claim or comparison which is directly or by implication misleading about the product advertised, or about any other product.

2.3 Advertisements should not contain any indication that the product advertised, or any ingredient, has some special quality or property which cannot be substantiated.

Denigration
3   Advertisements should not unfairly attack or discredit other products or advertisements directly or by implication.

Imitation
4.1 Advertisements should not imitate the devices, copy, slogans or general layout of advertisements for competing products in a way that is likely to mislead or confuse.

4.2 In the packaging and labelling of goods particular care should be taken to avoid causing confusion with competing products.

Scientific Terms and Statistics
5.1 Advertisements should not misuse scientific terms, statistics or quotations.

5.2 Scientific jargon and irrelevancies should not be used to make claims appear to have a scientific basis they do not possess.

5.3 Statistics with a limited validity should not be presented in such a way as to imply that their validity is greater than it really is.

Appeals to Fear
6   Advertisements should not without justifiable reason play on fear.

Superstition
7   Advertisements should not exploit the superstitious.

Safety
8   Advertisements should not without justifiable reason depict or describe situations which show dangerous practices or a disregard for safety. Special care should be taken in advertisements directed towards or depicting children.

Advertisements addressed to children
9 Advertisements addressed to children should not contain anything, whether in illustration or otherwise, which might result in harming them, physically, mentally or morally, or which exploits their credulity.

Testimonials
10.1 A testimonial used in an advertisement should be genuine, not more than three years old, and related to the experience of the person giving it.
10.2 Testimonials should not contain any statement or implication contravening the provisions of this Code.

Advertisements in editorial style
11 An advertisement should be clearly distinguishable from the editorial content of the publication in which it appears. It should therefore be so designed, produced and printed that it is immediately recognisable by the ordinary reader as an advertisement.
For further guidance see CAP Bulletin No. 6, Item 40.

'Free'
12 Goods or samples may be described as "free" if they are supplied at no cost or no extra cost (other than actual postage or carriage) to the recipient. A trial may be described as "free" although the customer is expected to pay the cost of returning the goods, provided that the advertisement makes clear the customer's obligation to do so.

Guarantees
13 Advertisements may contain the word "guarantee", "guaranteed", "warranty" or "warranted" or words having the same meaning only if the full terms of the guarantee are clearly set out in the advertisement or are made available to the purchaser in writing at the point of sale or supplied with the goods. The terms should include details of the remedial action open to a purchaser. No advertisements should contain a direct or

implied reference to a guarantee which takes away or diminishes the statutory or common law rights of a purchaser, unless the manufacturer assumes a contractual responsibility to the purchaser in extent at least equivalent to such rights.

Mail Order

14.1 Advertisements for goods offered by mail order should not be accepted unless:
   (a) the name of the advertiser is prominently displayed at the address given in the advertisement
   (b) adequate arrangements exist at that address for enquiries to be handled by a responsible person available on the premises during normal business hours
   (c) samples of the goods advertised are made available there for public inspection and
   (d) an undertaking has been obtained from the advertiser that money will be refunded in full to buyers who can show justifiable cause for dissatisfaction with their purchases or with delay in delivery.

14.2 Advertisers who offer goods by mail order should be prepared to meet any reasonable demand created by their advertising, and should be prepared to demonstrate or where practicable supply samples of the goods advertised to the media owners to whom their advertisements are submitted.

Direct Sale Advertising

15 Direct sale advertisements are not acceptable without adequate assurances from the advertiser and his advertising agency (a) that the products advertised will be supplied at the price stated in the advertisement within a reasonable time from stocks sufficient to meet potential demand, and (b) that sales representatives when calling upon persons responding to the advertisement will demonstrate and make available for sale the products advertised. It will be taken as prima facie

evidence of misleading and unacceptable "bait" advertising for the purpose of "switch selling" if an advertiser's salesmen seriously disparage or belittle the cheaper article advertised or indicate unreasonable delays in obtaining delivery or otherwise put difficulties in the way of its purchase.

Direct sale advertising is that placed by the advertiser with the intention that the products or services advertised, or some other products or services, shall be sold or provided at the home of any person responding to the advertisement.

Home visits by advertiser's representatives
16 Where it is the intention of an advertiser to send a representative to call on respondents to his advertisements (a) such fact must be apparent from the advertisement or from any particulars subsequently supplied and (b) the respondent must be given an adequate opportunity of refusing any such call.

Homework schemes
17 Advertisements for homework schemes should not be offered to media unless accompanied with full details of the work involved and of the conditions imposed on the homeworker.
"Homework scheme" means a scheme in which a person is invited to make articles or perform services at home for remuneration.

Inertia Selling
18 Advertisements should not be accepted from advertisers who supply goods without express authority.

Instructional courses
19.1 Advertisements offering courses of instruction should not promise or imply that persons completing such courses will obtain any particular employment or level of remuneration; nor offer unrecognised "degrees" or qualifications.
19.2 Advertisements for correspondence courses in

chiropody or any of the auxiliary services covered by the Professions Supplementary to Medicine Act 1960 (i.e. dietitians, medical laboratory technicians, occupational therapists, physiotherapists, radiographers and remedial gymnasts) should not be accepted.

Franchise schemes

20 Advertisements by franchisors seeking franchisees should not be accepted until the franchisor has provided all the information required by the media.

"Franchise scheme" means a scheme where a company, firm or individual (known as a franchisor) gives to a person (known as a franchisee) the right, often exclusive, to sell specified products or other specified services in a defined geographical area, or premises, in return for an initial payment and/or percentage of profits (or royalty).

For further guidance see CAP Bulletin No. 5, Item 38.

PART B. Medicines, Treatments and Appliances

These paragraphs apply in addition to those in part A.

This part of the Code applies to the advertising to the public of medicines, treatments and appliances for the prevention or alleviation of any ailment, illness or disease. It does not apply to advertisements published by or under the authority of a Government Ministry or Department, not to advertisements for medicines, treatment and appliances addressed directly to registered medical or dental practitioners, pharmacists, registered medical auxiliaries or nurses, sent direct or published in their respective professional or technical journals.

Illnesses requiring medical attention

21 Advertisements should not offer any medicine or treatment for serious diseases, conditions or complaints

which need the attention of a registered medical practitioner.

(*See in particular the list in Appendix II of the Code*)

Diagnosis or treatment by correspondence

22 Advertisements should not contain any offer to diagnose or to treat any ailment, illness or disease, or symptoms of ill-health by correspondence; nor invite information in order to advise on or prescribe treatment by correspondence.

References

CHAPTER 1

1. *Advertising*, Opposition Green Paper (The Labour Party, 1972).
2. *Report on the Supply of Household Detergents* (The Monopolies Commission, 1966) House of Commons Papers 105.

CHAPTER 2

1. V. Packard, *The Hidden Persuaders* (McKay, 1957).
2. J. K. Galbraith, *The Affluent Society* (Pelican, 1962).
3. —— *The New Industrial State* (Penguin, 1968).
4. O. J. Firestone, *The Economic Implications of Advertising* (Methuen, 1967) p. 35.
5. C. Wilson, *Unilever 1945–65* (Cassell, 1968) p. 101.
6. Quoted in R. Harris and A. Seldon, *Advertising and the Public* (Andre Deutsch, 1962).
7. A. Toynbee, 'Is Advertising Morally Defensible?' in R. J. Holloway and R. S. Hancock *The Environment of Marketing Behaviour*, 2nd ed. (John Wiley, 1969) chap. 24.
8. P. Doyle, 'Some Economic Aspects of Advertising', *Economic Journal* (1968).
9. For a fuller list see Firestone, op. cit.

CHAPTER 3

1. *Economist*, 11 Mar 1972, p. 20.
2. A. C. Pigou, *The Economics of Welfare* (London, 1920).

158 References

3. R. Harris and A. Seldon, *Advertising and the Public* (Andre Deutsch, 1962) p. 68.
4. Cited from A. Sedgwick, 'The Public Responsibility of the Advertiser', *Advertising Quarterly*, 29 (1971) p. 21.
5. Cited from W. Alderson, *Dynamic Marketing Behaviour* (Irwin, 1965) p. 60.
6. T. Veblen, *The Theory of the Leisure Class* (Macmillan, 1899).
7. P. Kotler, *Marketing Management* (Prentice-Hall, 1967) p. 88.
8. W. Taplin, *Advertising: a New Approach* (Hutchison, 1962) p. 19.
9. V. Packard, *The Hidden Persuaders* (McKay, 1957) p. 221.
10. M. Abramowitz, 'Resource and Output Trends in the US since 1870', *American Economic Review* (1956).
11. K. E. Boulding, *Economic Analysis*, 3rd ed. (1955) 672.
12. Sir D. H. Robertson, *Lectures on Economic Principles* (Staples, 1958) I, 169.

CHAPTER 4

1. W. J. Baumol, *Business Behaviour, Value and Growth* (Prentice-Hall, 1958).
2. P. J. Verdoorn, 'Marketing from the Producer's Point of View,' *Journal of Marketing* (Jan 1956) pp. 221–35.
3. J. Dean, *Managerial Economics* (Prentice-Hall, 1951).
4. O. E. Williamson, *The Economics of Discretionary Behaviour* (Prentice-Hall, 1964).
5. I. Feller, 'Production Isoquants and the Analysis of Technological and Technical Change', *Quarterly Journal of Economics* (1972).
6. P. Kotler, *Marketing Management*, 3rd ed. (Prentice-Hall, 1972) p. 677.
7. See T. Joyce, 'What Do We Know About How Advertising Works?', ESOMAR Seminar (1967).

CHAPTER 5

1. Daniel Starch, *Principles of Advertising* (A. W. Shaw Co., 1923).
2. *Gallup Ads of the Year, 1970* (The Gallup Poll).
3. W. A. Mindak, 'Fitting the Semantic Differential to the Marketing Problem', *Journal of Marketing* (1961).
4. See for example, J. E. Fothergill and A. S. C. Ehrenberg, 'On the Schwerin Analysis of Advertising Effectiveness', *Journal of Marketing Research* (1965).
5. J. P. Morris, *Road Safety Publicity: Quantifying the Effectiveness of Public Service Advertising*, Advertising Association Research Monograph No. 6 (1972) p. 69.
6. K. S. Palda, *The Measurement of Cumulative Advertising Effect* (Prentice-Hall, 1964).
7. L. G. Telser, 'Advertising and Cigarettes', *Journal of Political Economy* (1962).
8. Lambin, 'Measuring the Profitability of Advertising', *Journal of Industrial Economics* (1969).
9. W. J. Baumol, *Economic Theory and Operations Analysis*, 2nd ed. (Prentice-Hall, 1965) chap. 10.
10. R. E. Quandt, 'Estimating Advertising Effectiveness: Some Pitfalls in Econometric Methods', *Journal of Marketing Research* (1964).
11. T. Corlett, *An Introduction to the Use and Interpretation of Reading Frequency Data* (Institute of Practitioners in Advertising, 1967).

CHAPTER 6

1. W. Alderson, *Dynamic Marketing Behaviour* (Irwin, 1965) p. 119.
2. W. J. Baumol, *Economic Theory and Operations Analysis*, 2nd ed. (Prentice-Hall, 1965) p. 181.
3. G. Polanyi, *Detergents: a Question of Monopoly*, IEA Research Monograph No. 24 (1970) p. 20.
4. G. Stigler, 'The Economics of Information', *Journal of Political Economy* (1961).
5. P. Doyle, *Advertising Expenditure and Consumer Demand*, Oxford Economic Papers (1968).

CHAPTER 7

1. G. Polanyi, op. cit., pp. 35–6.
2. For example, R. W. Jastram, 'A Treatment of Distributed Lags in the Theory of Advertising Expenditure', *Journal of Marketing* (1955).
3. F. V. Waugh, 'Needed Research on the Effectiveness of Farm Products Promotions', *Journal of Farm Economics* (1962).
4. S. Hoos, 'The Advertising and Promotion of Farm Products:. Some Theoretical Issues', *Journal of Farm Economics* (1962).
5. L. G. Telser, 'Advertising and Competition', *Journal of Political Economy* (1964).
6. W. Taplin, *Advertising: A New Approach* (Hutchinson, 1962) pp. 95–6.
7. N. Kaldor, 'The Economic Aspects of Advertising', *Review of Economic Studies* (1949).
8. H. M. Mann, J. A. Henning and J. W. Meehan, 'Advertising and Concentration: An Empirical Investigation', *Journal of Industrial Economics* (1967).
9. 'Symposium on Advertising and Concentration', *Journal of Industrial Economics* (1969).
10. W. Duncan Reekie, 'Some Problems associated with the Marketing of Ethical Pharmaceutical Products', *Journal of Industrial Economics* (1970).
11. W. Duncan Reekie, *The Economics of Innovation with Special Reference to the Pharmaceutical Industry* (ABPI, 1971) p. 8.
12. W. S. Comanor and T. A. Wilson, 'Advertising, Market Structure and Performance', *Review of Economics and Statistics* (1967).
13. R. Dorfman and P. O. Steiner, 'Optimal Advertising and Optimal Quality', *American Economic Review* (1954).
14. See for example, Estes Kefauver, *In a Few Hands* (Pelican, 1966) pp. 74–7.
15. H. I. Ansoff, 'A Model for Diversification', *Management Science* (1958).
16. F. Harary and B. Lipstein, 'The Dynamics of Brand Loyalty: A Markovian Approach', *Operations Research* (1962).

CHAPTER 8

1. G. S. Becker, 'A Theory of the Allocation of Time', *Economic Journal* (1965).
2. 'Report on the Supply of Household Detergents' (The Monopolies Commission, 1966) House of Commons Papers 105.
3. Ibid., p. 44, para 125.
4. '... competition is restricted to the field of advertising and promotion. This not only results in wasteful expenditure but also deters potential competitors

who might, otherwise, provide a safeguard against excessive profits . . . If competition can be diverted from excessive advertising and promotion to prices, we believe that the result will be not only a saving in cost but also a more effective check upon profits.' Ibid., p. 43, para 121.

5. Polanyi, op. cit., p. 25.
6. Ibid., pp. 40—2.
7. 'It is difficult to see any reason, other than that the terms of entry are too onerous, why this profitable field should, *with the exception of liquid detergents*, have been left largely in the hands of the two companies . . . We are indeed a little surprised that multiple stores which market their own brands of liquid detergents do not as a rule market their own brands of powders.' House of Commons Papers 105, op. cit. p. 36, para 104. (my italics).
8. *Advertising*, Opposition Green Paper (The Labour Party, 1972), p. 56.
9. Ibid., p. 15.
10. J. Schumpter, *Capitalism, Socialism and Democracy* (New York: Harper, 1950) p. 88.
11. Ibid., p. 84.
12. J. L. Simon, *Issues in the Economics of Advertising* (University of Illinois Press, 1970) pp. 279—80.
13. Opposition Green Paper, op. cit., p. 55.
14. Cited from the *Daily Telegraph*, 7 Aug 1972.
15. Taplin, op. cit., p. 111.
16. D. Tarschys, 'The Demanding Consumer: Developments in Sweden', *Advertising Quarterly*, No. 28 (Summer 1971) 15.
17. Y. Brozen, 'The FTC and "Trial by Publicity" ', *Advertising Quarterly* No. 31 (Spring, 1972) 26—7.
18. Tarschys, op. cit., p. 20.
19. Economists' Advisory Group, p. 78.
20. Ibid., p. 77.
21. Ibid., p. 81.
22. Opposition Green Paper, op. cit., p. 3.
23. *Which* (Mar 1972) 66.
24. Opposition Green Paper, op. cit., p. 8.
25. Cited from *The Financial Times*, 16th July, 1973.

CHAPTER 9

1. J. K. Galbraith, *The New Industrial State* (Hamish Hamilton, 1967).
2. S. Brittan, *Government and Market Economy*, Hobert Paperback (Institute of Economic Affairs, 1971) p. 7.
3. J. K. Galbraith, *The Affluent Society* (Pelican, 1962) p. 131.
4. Nielsen Researcher (May—June, 1968).

Index

161